Carl H. A. Bjerregaard

**Lectures on Mysticism and Nature Worship**

Second Series

Carl H. A. Bjerregaard

**Lectures on Mysticism and Nature Worship**
*Second Series*

ISBN/EAN: 9783337285906

Printed in Europe, USA, Canada, Australia, Japan

Cover: Foto ©Andreas Hilbeck / pixelio.de

More available books at **www.hansebooks.com**

# LECTURES ON MYSTICISM

AND

## Nature Worship

---

SECOND SERIES

---

By C. H. A. BJERREGAARD

> —God! Thou art love! I build my faith on that.—
> —You must be merged in the Beloved to know the beauty of the Beloved.—

---

M. R. KENT
198 CUSTOM HOUSE PLACE, CHICAGO
1897

CORBITT & BURNHAM, PRINTERS
CHICAGO

## PREFACE

Most of the following lectures were delivered in Chicago, November 28-30, 1896, but they have been thoroughly revised and much enlarged for print.

I wish to express my thanks and gratitude to those friends who made it possible for me to go to Chicago. I regret that they desire to remain unnamed, but I agree with them, that ONLY BY SERVICE ARE WE PERFECTED.

C. H. A. BJERREGAARD.

# CONTENTS

*Preface.*—Uplift of Heart and Address.

*First Lecture.*—Motto. Pilgrims of the Infinite. The Fourth World. Vision of the Sephiroth. The Presence of the Woods. The Kabbalistic worlds and forces. Dionysius on how to unite.

*Second Lecture.*—Motto. Cry for Freedom. Heart and Soul-life. Faith. Jacobi. Appeal for spiritual life.

*Third Lecture.*—Motto. Music and Numbers. Idealism.

*Fourth Lecture.*—Motto. History in the Heavens. Lawlessness and Occultism. The Universal Ministry.

*Fifth Lecture.*—Motto. Universal Ministry. Religion of Jesus. Value of the Bible compared to Oriental Philosophy. Yogas. Decalogue, Lord's Prayer and Sermon on the Mount. Emblems and Symbols. Miss Farmer on Greenacre.

*Sixth Lecture.*—Motto. Invocation. The Human. Nature worship. Influence of the stars. Freedom. Merged in the Beloved.

*Seventh Lecture.*—Motto. Invocation. Nature worship. Pine trees and cones. Vortex. Cycles and Historical Development.

*Eighth Lecture.*—Love.

*Ninth Meeting.*—Questions and Remarks. Excursion to Mt. Salvat.

*Appendix* to Lectures on Nature worship and Love.

*Epilogue.*

## UPLIFT OF HEART.

*May that spirit of ours, which is a ray of perfect wisdom, pure intellect, and permanent existence, an inextinguishable light set in mortal bodies, recognize its glory and consciously become united with the Self, supremely blest! Thus shall we become "living souls."*

I trust the flowers that bloomed so recently have not been killed by winter frost, and that your enthusiasm has not burned out! You cannot worship (worth-ship) without fire and you ought not lay faded flowers on the eternal altar!

Do not allow the rudeness of vulgar circumstances to usurp the place which belongs to the Vision and do not give way to the petty details which clamor for the control of your soul! Withdraw regularly to the Secret and throw new and fresh sacrificial butter on the hearth, that the Log may burn. The log is your body and soul in their lower aspects, and it burns only when you *sacrifice!*

Be not afraid of what you call being too familiar with "The Beloved." Let not that temptation destroy the elevation of life you have attained. Can there be any too great familiarity between the bride and the bridegroom, between the soul and the Divine? No! No! "Nearer, nearer, my God, to Thee!" Your Beloved is no far off God, who is indifferent and who goes off occasionally on a trip to Ethiopia, leaving the world to Vortex. Your Beloved is a *present* God, the God of your heart and kidneys.

> I am my Beloved's,
> And his desire is toward me.

The New Age has come out of the ritualistic view, which supposed, that the Beloved demanded conventional forms as cards of admission to his heart, and loved not in fullness of body and soul and joy, but by means of symbols. Symbols of those days were idols, either in the form of priests or an oblation. There is nothing now between the bride and the Beloved. The veil is rent. Isis has raised her garment. The night is past and the Sun of Salvation shines gloriously in the sky.

The New Age does not speak in emblematic language. The breath, the sigh, from a pure heart moves the well of living waters and we may all drink.

> Eat, O friends;
> Drink, yea, drink abundantly of love!

The New Age hates the smell of burnt offerings; we stand no more in the signs of rams and goats. Zoolatry was in order for Israel and Egypt, but not for those who have realized their kinship to the Divine; not for those who are Sons of God and who commune early and late, whose every act is worship, and whose hearts are quick with Divine Life. The New Age does not look to a temple in Jerusalem or elsewhere. The whole world is our temple when we look outside. Our hearts within is our individual temple. Man is *the* temple. There is no outer and inner, no place more sacred and pure than another. The world is the garment of the Beloved. No High Priest and no door-keeper is needed, the holiness of instinct guides the bride.

The New Age keeps every day as a Sabbath-day, needs no set times for prayers and does not circumcise one flock and not another. The Holy Spirit makes every land a Holy Land and all the tribes of man may dwell in it.

Our God is Human. God, Jehovah is no more a dreadful name. Neither Doctors nor Scribes stand guard over it. We have seen the Divine face to face. He created us for His glory.

*It is the ground we do not tread upon which supports us.*
                                            *Taoist Wisdom.*

# FIRST LECTURE.

I do not want to address you by the conventional "Ladies and Gentlemen." It is out of place where we meet to "reason together" on Eternal Things.

I address you as Pilgrims of the Infinite, for you are pilgrims; I can see that on your faces. You are not pilgrims either *from* or *to* the Infinite, but you are *of* the Infinite. *From* and *to* indicate space and time relations, but in the Infinite we recognize neither time nor space; there is no to-day and to-morrow; no here and no there. Eternity is no farther off from the Mystic, than the moment in which he speaks. You are Pilgrims OF the Infinite, which indicates a peculiar relationship, one of SAMENESS, one which far surpasses anything ordinary thought can conceive.

I come to you the second time—for what purpose? To lecture! No! I come as a Fellow pilgrim to SPEAK to you, to address you and call upon you to come to look upon the pictures of the Infinite, I have to show.

I feel the same harmonious condition in this hall as when I spoke to you in the Spring. You were then in an attitude of peace and rest and the smiles on your faces now, indicate that you again are in the Highest. I feel encouraged by your smiles, for they prophesy nothing but Good.

I need all your goodness and your peace, for I shall speak from a standpoint that can only be maintained by your support. Referring you to this diagram, I shall speak from a standpoint here indicated as the Fourth World.

Matter:                           Soul:
    Solid.                             Vegetable.
    Fluent.                          Animal.
    Gaseous.                      Human.
    Fourth form.               Fourth form.
Spirit:               Fourth form:
    Knowing.                     First form.
    Willing.                        Second form.
    Loving.                         Third form.
    Fourth form.              Fourth form.

The Fourth form can never be entered except in states of quietness and peace. For the time being we must absolutely remove all distressing thoughts and perplexities. The Fourth form is Heart Life, is Soul Life.

In the Spring, I gave you numerous definitions of this plane by quoting the Mystics. Let me to-day add one by a modern. In his "Science of Religion" Max Müller, speaking of this plane as a faculty, says:

"There is in man a faculty which I call simply the faculty of apprehending the Infinite, not only in religion, but in all things; a power independent of sense and reason, a power in a certain sense contradicted by sense and reason, but yet, I suppose, a very real power, if we see how it has held its own from the beginning of the world, how neither sense nor reason have been able to overcome it, while it alone is able to overcome both reason and sense."

Still another expression is this by Sophie Germain, in Ravaisson: Philosophie.)

"There is within us a profound sense of unity, order, and proportion, which serves to guide all our judgment. In moral subjects we find in it the rule of right; in intellectual, the knowledge of the truth; in matters of taste, the character of beauty."

Those who were not here in the spring I refer to the printed lectures and ask them to read up for themselves. We shall not have time to go over that ground again. The plane we want to enter is the Soul- and Heart-Life.

You are all perfectly familiar with those first forms,—Matter, Spirit and Soul. You all know the three forms of Matter, Solid, Fluent and Gaseous, and also those of the Spirit, Knowing and Willing and Loving, and also those of the Soul, Vegetable Animal and Human. Each one of those has a fourth one, with which you are somewhat familiar, although not consciously. You are living in it. I will give you an illustration which I think will cover the whole ground. When you write a letter to a friend or to a lover,—to somebody in whom you are intensely interested, you instinctively throw yourselves into that letter. You may write a great many words that in themselves are expressive of something and tell their own story, but the one that receives that letter gets, alongside of that, another thing: gets that love which you laid on the surface of the paper, the Something which was not penned in the words and was nowhere located on this or the other line, but is wound in with it and exudes from it. The friend that receives the letter reads it and sees all the facts and data and declarations that are made, and when he or she lays down the letter, then comes an influx (or efflux) from that letter, and that is the spiritual influence that you put in that letter. You are all aware of this. You have been working in the Fourth World. You must not come here in an intellectual state. You are not here this morning to get any information which is directly to give the much-coveted POWER. You shall get that power, we all are seeking, but you shall get it only by devoting yourselves to that Heart and Soul Life which I shall urge upon you and which we, you and I, shall show in these meetings. You see, I am addressing myself to the fourfold office, as I defined it in the spring; I am taking it for granted that you know where you are in colors and that you have those ministries developed in you. It is on the fourth plane, the Mystic Life is lived. It is not occult but mystical. You will remember I have defined the difference between the two, between the attainment of power by processes of knowledge and the attainment of power and influence by perfect freedom.

A letter of the kind I have been describing, you cannot write unless you are free; that is, unless there are no disturbances between the two, the one that is writing and the one that is receiving; there must be perfect peace and harmony between the two, or you cannot throw this spirit into the letter. You can throw into a letter the spirit of fact and criticism, etc., which also lies on the surface, but it is of an intellectual character. But this one thing that I want to urge, that you have not thought of before, you can only produce when you let your love nature have the best of you for the time being; you can call it heart-, soul-, or love-life, I do not care what you call it, but it is this, the Fourth—I have written no name in either of the spheres. You can call it by the name of Energy or by any name from eastern or western philosophy, no matter. To give a general clue to that whole life, I should say it is Fire-life. I can best express it for myself in terms of Fire. If you will examine yourselves, you will no doubt feel and have found by observation, that in passing through your lowest states, if they have been deeply sensuous, in those sensuous-degrees that you would not openly acknowledge, that the Fire life raged wildly. It exists in all of the states of Matter, Spirit and Soul, but particularly in the fourth form. I call it Fire life, and there is one way I can help you to live and see it. Will you all turn toward the sun* and hold your hands with the fingers together, as I show you, and place them over your eyes so that the sun's rays will not destroy the optic nerve. Let the sun shine through your fingers, through the transparent part of the fingers. Do this and report to me what you have seen and we will make some comparisons. Keep your eyes open and see through your hand. Stare directly into the burning furnace of the sun. You may consider the sun physical, spiritual or otherwise, it is immaterial. Throw yourselves into the best mood of heart and soul, or an emotional attitude, and then tell me what you have seen. Let nobody observe anyone else; be absolutely unknown to and not recognizing your neighbor. I will go out of the Hall for a few minutes. . . .

Now that you have done this, will those of you who have found your positions in the Four, rise. You need not tell us what you

*The audience turned to the sun, just then shining brightly into the hall.

saw or perceived. And now the others who have had any distinct perceptions will please rise.

A member: I think some of us do not understand your meaning.

The lecturer: I mean those of you who have recognized your fourfold office in the spring. Those of you who know where you are, either in the Apostolic, Prophetic, Evangelistic or Pastoral quality,—those, if they have seen anything, will please rise.

(Several members arose.)

The lecturer: You must not tell anybody what you have seen. I will warn you,—if you have seen anything that you could describe, then it is worth nothing, and you should experiment over again. If it takes a definite form so you can describe it, it is not what you want. What you should receive is an influx. You will be able to receive it if you will hold your hand as I show you,— perhaps you have not understood what I mean,—when you hold your hand up and let the sun shine through it, you know how it glows. Looking through that glowing flesh you shall be able to travel up those rays of the sun that enter your hand and you can follow those powers that are yours by affinity into those four worlds respectively. But neither of those four worlds is so material that you can describe them in any way. You may describe them to yourself, that will be all right,—you must have a definite conception; but if you can reduce it to a formula to give to another, your vision is not worth anything. How many of those who arose had such conception? If any of you had them I would say to them, continue those experiments, when the sun is beating right straight on your face, particularly at high noon. There will come a time sooner or later, and perhaps you have already had it now, that you shall see not only yourself in those rays, but you shall see visions such as Jacob had, of angels ascending and descending,—not angels in bodies with wings, etc., no, you shall see powers moving and that in the colors of the four. The seeing of all that is not the seeing of the eyes, or the brain, but is the seeing of your heart. The heart-life has an intellectual side, and that is the side you want to develop; in it is the true mystical life, or as I also call it, the personal or the human life; it centers there; and that is this fourth world we are so anxious to enter. Those of you who are in your fourfold office shall not only find your place in the cosmological make-up of the universe, but you shall actually see yourselves in the back. I think I have spoken of it before. There is a mystery in the way we are made. We are always going forward, never going back; we are the ultimates of divine rays. When you come into your office you shall be able to turn yourself around and see the fiery rays that strike the back of your head. Having attained that, you shall have the much-coveted power; and the best of it is that you shall have that power in a form that will make it harmless to others and beneficial to yourself. Many of the other powers you know, attained by breathing, taking drugs and all those many queer methods, that are recommended, are dangerous; they will sooner or later turn against you; but powers attained this way can never turn against you, or be injurious or ruinous. It is a source from which you will literally draw life,—literally take it up and feed on it, and you shall be able to climb up over those "golden stairs" that the mystics talk so much about; it is not a fable or allegory. The reason for this is that life thus descends in an orderly way; but the powers attained by the mere occult methods do not come in an orderly way. You will please understand I am not here to attack anybody; when now speaking against certain occult practices, I am not having anybody in mind whom I am aiming at and attacking either openly or indirectly; I am not in conflict with anybody; I have come in a peaceful spirit and will not be misunderstood as if I were saying anything against anybody here. I want to make a distinction between what I call ordinary occult methods and the mystical methods. If I say anything that sounds hard or critical you will please understand that it is done only for the purpose of bringing out by contrast the world I wish to lead you into. Our Heart-life, as I said before, has features that ordinarily are not understood. It is not understood ordinarily that we can read and write and talk and examine things by the heart; it seems so irrational to people, that they will oppose it and say they do it with their brain. How can you do it with your brain? You are not understanding any more by your brain than by your finger-tips. You generally think you are doing it through the nerve-centers in your brain; but the key to your life is in the heart, not in the brain. The brain can be removed and can wither away and still life goes on. All the best work you have done and do do, the love that now shines on your faces, is not brain work, it is heart and soul life.

There is another way in which you may perceive the great and glorious life that lies abroad and is everywhere, the life of the Fourth Plane. The next time you go into the woods, go into some place among the trees where they stand thick enough to prevent your seeing the sky on the other side; you can easily find such a place, no matter whether among the pines or the leaf trees; stand perfectly still, look in among the trees, hold your eyeballs still; not exactly staring; look intently but hold your eyeballs still. Some of you may have to hold your breath in order to hold your eyeballs still, but a very little practice will soon enable you to do so. In a second or two,—certainly within a minute,—you shall perceive something. You shall perceive the spirit of that wood; it will appear before you; the spirit of the wood is living there as vigorously and personally as you live, and, your contact with it is as real as with any human individual. You understand what I mean when I say PERSONAL contact with another human individual. The best influences that you receive from your friends, or neighbors, or whoever you meet with, or talk to, is not that which they say or do, but the personal efflux that comes from them; it is that which you perceive and appreciate, feel and love, and is that which makes the sympathetic bond between them and yourself. Such a presence as you thus perceive in your neighbor, such a presence you shall perceive in the woods and all these things belong to the sphere of soul-life, heart-life, that I talked of. It is a fact that a villain can also throw out an atmosphere and we feel his presence, but he is not throwing it out with love, or perfectly; they are "crooked" vibrations those that come from him— the others are "straight,"—or, as I prefer to say, orderly; they have come through a gradual descent, through different degrees of this angelic world through which we are connected with the Almighty, the Great One, the Great Being, and they were all given in the spring lectures; but it was not said there what the connection was between those higher orders and yourselves; that I left out last spring, but I shall attempt to give it this time.

Now I will ask for questions.

A member: In using the word "seeing" or "perceiving" in looking into the depths of the woods, was it in the sense of vibration?

The lecturer: I should have defined myself more closely. By "seeing," of course, I did not mean merely seeing, as we ordinarily understand it, viz., throwing ourselves on an object and examining it in the light of either of the three forms as represented on the diagram. You know I warned you against that.

It has been asked again and again, What shall I do to enter this world, or to stay in it, to live in it? I should give as a general rule this formula: "Live in the idea of the thing." Those of you who are artists, all those who in any way have been working with the plastic powers of life will know what I mean. Suppose you were an architect; when planning your house you built it in your mind, as you know, and of astral matter. You had the whole house fully perfected in all its forms, standing there in your mind, and what you did afterward was to reduce that mental house to an expression on the paper. When you make a design, reduce your idea of the thing, or the arcane, the "schema" of it, to a presentation on the paper. If you can enter into the spiritual conception of such a presentation and hold the idea in your mind and stay in it, you are then in "the idea of it," and in the Fourth World.

A member: You mean that we should live in our ideals.

The lecturer: Yes, you may put it in that way. You may

have some difficulty with the word idea. I am not taking it in the sense as meaning merely a notion of the thing, which is the ordinary sense of the word; I take it in the good old Platonic sense as the type, the plastic form, the model. You are more or less familiar with the Platonic idea, I suppose. Now stay in the idea of the thing, and you have found the way of the mystic life. You have an idea of your friends, and it is really that idea you are clinging to and not your friend. So long as that idea is not disturbed or polluted, your friendship lasts. These are things you are all familiar with but things you do not understand consciously. Make this a matter of understanding and stay in the ideas, then you are mystics and occultists, and there is not a thing in existence, all the way from infinite Being to the most minute particle, that you are not familiar with. That is all there is to the mystic ways of entering things.

Now please look at this diagram:

THE FOURFOLD OR FOUR DIMENTIONAL LIFE:

| Matter: | solid<br>fluent<br>gaseous<br>4th form | corresponds to | Aziah, the world of action—<br>—apostles control— |
|---|---|---|---|
| Spirit: | knowing<br>willing<br>loving<br>4th form | —"— | Yetzirah, the world of formation—<br>—prophets reveal— |
| Soul: | vegetative<br>animal<br>human<br>4th form | —"— | Briah, the world of creation—<br>—evangelists proclaim— |
| 4th form | 1 form<br>2 "<br>3 "  } all fire<br>4 " | —"— | Atziloth, the archetypical world—<br>—pastors guide— |

17

My object is to point out the cosmological parallels to the psychological states I gave you in the Spring. You all know the Kabbalistic terms of the diagram.

As I said:

Matter is known as solid, fluent, gaseous, and under a fourth form.

Spirit is known as knowing, willing, loving, and under a fourth form.

Soul is known as vegetative, animal, human, and under a fourth form.

These fourth forms are of Being, which means Wholeness Divinity, etc. To these three existences Matter, Spirit and Soul comes also a fourth existence, which also is divided into four forms, but their names are not even known to-day.

To Matter answers the Kabbalistic world Aziah, more particularly that unnamed fourth form mentioned above, which expresses the World of Action.

To Spirit answers the Kabbalistic world Yetzirah, more particularly that unnamed fourth form mentioned above, which expresses the World of Formation.

To Soul answers the Kabbalistic world Briah, more particularly that unnamed fourth form mentioned above, which expresses the World of Creation.

To the fourth existence, also referred to above, and, which is also divided into four forms, answers the Kabbalistic archetypical world, Atziloth.

The real sphere of Apostolic activity lies in the world of Aziah, the World of Action.

The real sphere of Prophetic activity lies in the world of Yetzirah, the World of Formation.

The real sphere of Evangelistic activity lies in the world of Briah, the World of Creation.

The real sphere of Pastoral activity lies in the world of Atziloth, the archetypical world.

I have already in the Spring-lectures given you the Dionysian hierarchies. Let us now study them in the light of the four worlds and we shall see how wonderfully everything corresponds and we shall learn to do our work. You will each for yourself understand the mystery of your place in the universal man and also your work. It is very useful on general principles to compare the nine orders of the three hierarchies of Dionysius to the Sephiroth. By so doing we shall get a great deal of life wisdom. According to the vision of Dionysius, immediately upon the Trinity—Kether—come Seraphim, "all flaming and on fire," then Cherubim, "glorious beings of light, shining in nature." The Seraphim are "wise lovers" and correspond to Binah, Intelligence. The Cherubim are "loving wisdoms" and correspond to Chokhmah, Wisdom. We place ourselves in communion with the first by "our universal charity" and with the second by "divine wisdom." The Seraphim and Cherubim unite in the Thrones or Seats, the third order of the first hierarchy, who themselves also are wise, loving and "kingly;" they correspond to Tiphereth, Kingly Beauty. We commune with them by "being just."

In the second hierarchy we see first Dominations, "an express image of the true and archetypal dominion in God;" they correspond to Geburah, Strength. The next order is Virtues, in which are "zeal and care and energy, that all things in God may be strongly and manfully valiant in chaste and masculine virtue." They correspond to Chesed, Mercy. With the first we commune by "self control;" with the second by "compassion for suffering." Dominations and Virtues unite in the Powers, which "exhibit in themselves the divine unity, simplicity, power and authority." They, too, correspond to Tiphereth, Kingly beauty. We commune with the Powers by "resisting temptations."

The third hierarchy, the last, consists of Princedoms, Archangels and Angels. The first, "an image of the true and exalted principality in God" corresponds to Hod, Splendor. The second, "a certain supreme, wise and virtuous power" corresponds to Netzach, victory; the third order, Angels, are "tiding bringers" and the ultimate result of all the emanations, hence so beautifully corresponding to Yesod, Foundation. As all the Sephiroth unite and coalesce in Malkhuth, the Kingdom, so the Hierarchies are a Unit. With the Princedoms, we commune by humility, or with the Archangels, by "the study of the Divine Law;" with the Angels, by obedience. The Sephiroth are not only objective forms of Being, they are the very Ground of our individual existence. They are "the Primordial or Archetypal Man," the "Heavenly Man," in us. In another arrangement you will find this occult teaching in the following diagram:

| The fourfold Office. | Kabbalistic names for the four worlds and their characteristics. | | The Hierarchies of Dionysius and the means by which they are reached. |
|---|---|---|---|
| | | | (This hierarchy lies beyond human reach.) |
| Pastor. — Harmony. | Atziloth or archetypical world, or | The World of Divine Names — The World of Sephiroth — | *Seraphs*, communed with by universal love. *Cherubs*, communed with by elevation of soul to Divine Wisdom. *Thrones*, communed with by justice. |
| Prophet. — Purity. | Yetzirah or formative world, or | The World of Cherubin — | *Dominions*, communed with by command of self. *Virtues*, communed with by compassion for suffering. *Powers*, communed with by resisting temptations. |
| | | | *Princedoms*, communed with by humility. |
| Evangelist. — Richness. | Briah or creative world, or | The World of Archangels — | *Archangels*, communed with by zeal in studying the Divine Law. |
| Apostle. — Power. | Aziah or material world, or | The World of Planets and Daemons — | *Angels*, communed with by obedience. |

Kether, or the Crown, is the head; Chokhmah, Wisdom, is the brain; Binah, Intelligence, is the heart or the understanding. These three form "the head." Chesed, Mercy or Love is the right arm. Geburah, Strength, the left arm. Tiphereth, Beauty, is the chest. These three form the second triad. Netzach, Firmness, Victory, is the right leg. Hod, Splendor, is the left leg. Yesod, Foundation, is the genital organs. These three form the third triad. All nine Sephiroth, or three triads, are harmonized in Malkhuth, the Kingdom. Next time I meet you, I hope to be able to give you the practical application of this. I have not been able to finish the diagrams necessary. I do not know that anybody has presented to the world any study in this line, but though I stand single with my results and may have made mistakes, I shall not hesitate when the time comes, to publish that which I here give only in hints.

*The Philosophic vindication of Faith is the proof of the impossibility of comprehending all things in a reasoned system of knowledge.*
—*Fraser's Berkeley, in Philos. Classics.*

# SECOND LECTURE.

I hear throughout creation a cry for freedom. Everywhere mankind is sighing and from pole to pole there comes a groan of travail from the brute creation. Even inanimate creation voices the longings of the superior orders of being. The solemn night is mournful and the sea is melancholy; the sighing pine and the sobbing wave on the beach cry for redemption; the tropical forest is lonesome and the vast prairies look longingly to the pale moon; the majestic mountain rises in mute appeal to heaven, but cannot enter, and in the deep mines despair broods over an eternal darkness. In all these forms of creation, I see the same as I see in the deep and lonesome eye of the dog and the horse and the cow; they all call for freedom and for liberation. They are chained by Necessity and they sigh for the freedom of man's glorious kingdom: his ideal self.

Though man is called to freedom and is free by birthright he is nevertheless in bondage. *He has bound himself voluntarily* and he too cries for freedom. How is he to get it?

In the first place he IS free, I said, hence the first thing for him to do is to realize that fact. He must realize that he never was anything but saved; that he always was saved; that God is to be had for the asking. Next, he must take possession of that freedom.

The realization is no intellectual process, it is mystical rather. He must, as I said in the Spring lectures, re-collect himself and then in Meditation he will attain Union with God. The attainment of Union with God is freedom or realization of Self.

I shall not now repeat what I said in the Spring. At that time I quoted the Mystics. To-day I will quote a modern philosopher, Jacobi. Chalybæus said of him: "He showed that there is something more in our soul than a dead and empty mechanism of logical thinking and shadowy representations; he reassured us of *a deeper, and, as yet, an inviolable, treasure in the human spirit;* and, although this boon be hidden in the sevenfold veil of Isis, yet has he powerfully excited us to the investigation of it, by pointing to the reality of so precious a germ."

This deeper and yet unrealized treasure in the human spirit is *freedom*, freedom realized by the feelings; not feelings in the common vulgar sense as feelings of body, but *spiritual perceptions*.

Said Jacobi: "There is light in my heart, but it goes out whenever I attempt to bring it into the understanding. Which is the true luminary of these two? That of the understanding, which, though it reveals fixed forms, shows behind them only a bottomless gulf? Or that of the heart, which points its light promisingly upward, though determinate knowledge escapes it? Can the human spirit grasp the truth unless it possesses these two luminaries united in one light?"

In the former address, I emphasized very strongly the heart life because I want you to cultivate it. You are top-heavy with knowledge, with understanding. You need a great deal of ballast, and the ballast you need is Heart, Soul, Love-Life.

You have realized that in the understanding lies imbedded all the laws or forms of existence, and you have probably also discovered that through the understanding we enter into a bottomless deep of wisdom and marvels. But you want to acquire an equal realization of the heart as the source whence all influx flows, as the bridal chamber in which the human ego meets the Divine. Its light is dim, but its power is eternal. You cannot define its charms, but you are richer than before every time your heart has acted. Your understanding leads you out and away from yourself, but your heart builds a home and in Home are the gates of heaven. You want to realize this before you can attain the much-coveted power, divine power. But there is still more to do before you are a perfected man, before you can TAKE POSSESSION of Power. You must unite Heart and Understanding. The Divine is a Unit. You must become a Unit. The two must be UNITED, *not simply come together in union*. The human ego does not live as Immerman's Captain. This officer had served both Napoleon and the Germans; from both he had received numerous decorations and he had collected a vast mass of memorials of his campaigns. After the war, he did not know where his sympathies were the strongest, so he fitted up one room in his house in which he kept all Napoleonic souvenirs and another in which he kept the German mementoes, and lived alternately in the one and the other room, being now Napoleonic, now German. The human ego cannot live that way.

The same Jacobi, whom I quoted, also solves the problem he propounds. To him immediate and mediate knowledge unite in one, in the "deeper, and, as yet inviolable treasure in the human spirit." The Mystics call it God in the Ground of the soul, as I told you in the Spring. Jacobi understands it to be *freedom*, and so do I. It is to me that Heart and Soul-life which I locate in the Fourth World. The key to it is Trust, Faith.

I cannot speak enough for the Fourth Form; I cannot bring it often enough before you, because you need it. Not only do I speak from this standpoint, but I want to be understood to be doing so. Much of that which I say will have no meaning if not thus understood.

I am not speaking science as now understood. The science I care for, and which I study, is that of the heart. I want to know the workings of the spirit in me, and so do you. Influx is from above and not from below. If we know the laws of influx from the Deity, we can begin to acquire power and take possession of our heritage from eternity. Modern science—all science—equips man, but does not guide him to heaven. It teaches him ebb and flood in the sea, but not the currents of his own heart life. It leaves night in his heart. Science is reasoning from one (so-called) fact to another, but as we never can get that point outside our world which Archimedes asked for, and which is necessary for the true science, our reasoning, or our science can never be more than merely something very relative, a driving round in a circle. The farther we reach in knowledge, the farther we come in duality; even into manifoldness, and—*farther away from the spiritual reality*, we desire to attain. The mystic does not want cognitions of objects, he wants to transcend the relations of subject and object. We want consciousness, but we do not want to *have* consciousness. We want knowledge, but we do not want *to have* knowledge. The two states are diametrically opposite. You want to remember this, especially when you retire into the silence. I fear that many of you never come there. You bring something with you, while the secret is that you shall leave everything behind you. You must go out of this world, changing as it is, like the clouds, and enter That which it symbolizes.

There is one truth that has become very clear to me, year by year, and that is that I must live and do live by Trust, Faith. It is a truth I have not come to by any intellectual reasoning, nor is it a result of a lively instinct. I say lively, for an instinct there is, no doubt, behind it, but that instinct is not lively.

It is hard and persistent experience, which has taught me to live by Faith, in Trust; and you can easily see that it is so, that we must live by faith, when you hear my argument.

I know nothing of and cannot know the purposes of the Divine. I can speculate and in my own wisdom propound wonderful theories. I can, under the influence of passionate desire, make myself believe that the future is mine. In conceit I can dictate to the Divine what to do. But all comes to Naught. The wonderful scheme of history leaves nations and individuals free to act and to work out their individual purposes to the uttermost, but the Divine Will reaches its own purpose after all. And what that is we do not know. I throw myself absolutely upon the belief that Everything is for the best. I know, that every time I have had my own will on important subjects, subjects involving the highest ethical problems, I have chosen the wrong thing and suffered for it. I know also that Everything that has *come to me*, which *was given to me*, was the only thing worth having, *the thing* I needed. That which is worth anything to me now, that which I prize, that which has been of universal use to me, is a gift. Numerous factors in my life, entanglements, and troubles, are all of my own choosing, of my own will. Am I therefore wrong in giving up *my will* and saying "Thy purposes be fulfilled," a more literal meaning of the Lord's prayer: Thy will be done? Do not understand that this philosophy has made me a fatalist, or, that I am indifferent in acting. Nay! I try to walk cautiously, I look up and inquire daily: "Is this it?" I do try to carry out the lesson of the birds under heaven and the lilies of the fields. I am neither a bird, nor a lily, but a man and that means a compound of many elements. Being a man, I cannot stand still as the lily does and wait for the "early and late rain," for sunshine, etc., but I can acquire the stillness of the lily, I can introduce a certain simplicity into my life, etc., and that is Trust. Faith. In quietness and peace is our salvation. "Not by power, or by might, but by my spirit," said the Lord.

Like yourself, I have my melancholic states in which I cannot come to rest with anything in this world. I am so dreadfully alone. I long, I yearn for the Universal. I look into all the faces I meet for a soul that can satisfy my call. I cry, but hear no response. Shall I therefore think myself alone and fling myself into despair? Nay, I have learned, like the lily in the Spring, just before budding into flower, to know that this melancholy arises in the new life, that seeks freedom of expression. I feel powers in my soul, too strong for expression, so they revert upon me and for the time I suffer. Be quiet, like the lily! Soon you will find your work!

Like yourself, I have burned with intense longing to know the Truth and be done with the false images of Mâyâ. If I have become restless, I have only become entangled in some notion or other, in some philosophical system, eastern or western, and—I went away from the Truth. Now, when this great longing arises, I close my eyes to all ephemeral things and notions. I sweep out everything human and by and by a new life dawns upon me. Like the lily, I open my chalice to the Sun and I drink from the universal source.

Like yourself, I sometimes suffer agony when I come to realize my ignorance and sin. I call for redemption. Does it come by external means? Never! I seem to grow in mud. I draw my nourishment from dark earth and I breathe poisonous air. I am utterly miserable, for I see no redemption. But the redeemer liveth in the soul! After a while I see myself like a lily, whose very existence is drawn from the mud and dark earth and whose purity and high stalk is made from the carbon of the poisoned air it breathes. Then I thank the Great Being, whose manifestation is in *opposite* elements: who makes both light and darkness! I see evil transformed into good! I see mud, but a lily coming out of it! Then I understand that the Great Being is a wise gardener.

With these experiences, should I not trust? Why will I be

impatient? Impatience withers the soul more than old age and disease.

Now as to knowledge. What do *we know?* Nothing about the real nature of things! That which we call knowledge is only a result of possiting some one experience as a fact, and then reasoning from that fact. But such knowledge is not knowledge; it is only our ideas. But as we never can get beyond such notions, why should we be restless and worry? As Fichte has truly said, "All we need to know is God, freedom and immortality," so I believe it is. And these three facts we have by immediate consciousness. No mediate consciousness has given them to us, nor can it prove them after we got them. Let us then rest and trust! The time will come when we shall know, if it be so best!

Let us stay in and with Trust, it is the very door to Divinity. There a well opens with rich waters to quench the thirst of the soul. The moment you have learned to narrow down your philosophy to that state or condition, I call Trust, you will find that the world opens up on the other side of existence. The first plane you enter is the Fourth World, I have spoken about.

Can I not prevail upon you to come to Rest? You say you want to come to the Universal Consciousness, to Union with God, etc. You will come there by Trust. You cannot follow the mystic method, so fully described in the Spring, except you trust! You cannot enter that Universal Ministry you are called to, except by Trust, and you cannot work in it, except in Trust!

Will you overcome yourself?

"There is ever a song somewhere, my dear;
   There is ever a something sings alway:
There's the song of the lark when the skies are clear,
   And the song of the thrush when the skies are gray.
The sunshine showers across the grain,
   And the bluebird thrills in the orchard tree;
And in and out, when the eaves drip rain,
   The swallows are twittering ceaselessly.

There is ever a song somewhere, my dear,
   Be the skies above or dark or fair,
There is ever a song that our hearts may hear—
There is ever a song somewhere, my dear—
   There is ever a song somewhere!

There is ever a song somewhere, my dear,
   In the midnight black or the midday blue;
The robin pipes when the sun is here,
   And the cricket chirrups the whole night through.
The buds may blow and the fruit may grow,
   And the autumn leaves drop crisp and sear;
But whether the sun, or the rain, or the snow,
   There is ever a song somewhere, my dear.

There is ever a song somewhere, my dear,
   Be the skies above or dark or fair,
There is ever a song that our hearts may hear—
There is ever a song somewhere, my dear—
   There is ever a song somewhere!"

## THIRD LECTURE.

In continuation of the morning lectures I will bring up another standpoint from which you can enter the plane of the Fourth Dimension. I will give some other material with which to work, so that you can see yourself,—and that which I shall now say will be useful particularly to those of you who are musical. But I must make this confession before I go on with my talk, that I myself am not musical, and that you may hear some curious statements that will convince you of my utter incapacity for talking on the subject, that I have undertaken to talk upon, but I cannot help it, whatever I know of it, little or much, must be stated, and you must take it as it is, and I must stand the criticism. The fact is, that if I can convey to you the spiritual, or the soul-meaning of numbers, you can hereafter use those numbers with moral effect. That is, instead of counting one, two, three, four, etc.,—instead of merely counting those numbers, I want you to express the sense they contain; I want you to have before your mind not the number concept, but a vision of their spiritual content, a certain image which represents that number. When you are playing your scale, let moral conceptions run along with the scale; it is then inevitable that those who hear the music must perceive that life that flows with that music, because you cannot now any more play that music as mere mathematics. I am sorry that most music is so little more than a mathematical performance. Music should not be so, and was not so in the Beginning. It was then a moral factor in the human life.

I must say that I have before presented this subject to musical people, and they have agreed with me that there is something in it worth studying; a method by which they could not only find themselves, but communicate moral truths to those who listen to them. There are in New York some musicians who were at Greenacre last summer, where I first spoke of it, some who are experimenting and practicing on this line. I came to this thing in the year 1864, during the Schleswig-Holstein war, and right outside of my native city Fredericia, where is located one of the largest estates, in the possession of our family. I went there quite often as a scout and spy among the enemy, both in the day and night time, and I spent days among the Hungarians who were located there. These Hungarians had the habit in the evening of coming together in the large court yard, somebody would strike up a tune and they would all fall in and sing, sometimes the whole brigade of five thousand men, without any conductor. You can readily understand what an enormous volume of tune came from those five thousand throats, and from those souls, and that it had an overpowering effect on a sensitive soul. The Hungarians are perhaps the most musical people in the world. Those men were the enemies of my country and I was among them to find out what they were trying to do, yet those men completely overpowered me and carried me along with them. I heard in that music THE HUMAN ELEMENT. As I said this morning, it was not merely the sound of those human throats singing a melody, there was something entirely different there, the human element had so peculiar an effect that I, as I told you, an enemy among them, was completely carried out of myself, and for the moment forgot myself as a Dane. Later in life I have heard it repeatedly. When we in the regiments train the men to learn the signals we usually take them out on the drill-ground away from the city with a corporal and a trumpeter,— the trumpeter is there to sound the signal and the corporal to attend to order; the trumpeter plays the signal, and the men sing it to certain words, which express its meaning. They are usually men coming fresh from the fields, country boys, etc., who, as a rule, have had no training whatsoever; they sing whether they have a tune in them or not; most of them have no tune whatever, *but the less tune the more human life there is in it.* If you listen to them a thousand feet or two off you would hear the human element rather than the signal. I have never heard it when near the men, but when I went to the other end of the drill-ground and then listened, I could hear that peculiar sound, the universal element. These signals sung by the men always produced a moral effect upon me; I mean a soul-effect. I use "moral" because it is customary to speak of that whole world I refer to as the moral world,— but as I have used the terms heart- and soul-life I will now say it had a heart and soul effect. The notes created a peculiar effect and put me in certain states where I could have done almost anything along that line of vibration that came from the sound. When another trumpet would be sounded, and another signal would be given and the men singing that, another feeling would be created. These, my feelings, I could in a certain sense SEE, I could manifest them before myself. I was under the influence of those trumpets in the same way as old cavalry horses are. I don't know whether any of you have been on a drill-ground and seen the old cavalry or artillery horses answer to the signal. The raw recruit cannot control the horse, the horse knows the signal and obeys, and they teach the recruit that way;—they always put him on old horses. The moment a certain signal is sounded, the horse will obey that and cannot possibly do anything else, it never fails.

This is an exact parallel to what took place in me and what takes place in you if you will observe yourself. I am perfectly sure that the next time you hear a band going through the streets, if you will observe the effect of the various instruments upon you, you can easily single them out. You will find certain peculiar thrills going through you with certain peculiar notes. If you next time will be on the watch, you will very easily in your own way be able to translate the music into some words that express certain feelings. That will be what I call the soul effect, and that will bring you into this fourth world that I spoke of this morning.

Now we will go through the scale.

There is One. I will call that Being. By the One you should have a mental picture before yourselves of Being, without any characteristics, not the Becoming, but the simple indifferentiated Being, the All, the Universal. In sounding the note which in your scale would be the One, you will, after a little while, or perhaps at once, by that note, convey the idea of Being to those who listen to it. One has that effect. That is what it stands for in soul-life.

One then is Self, the Great All, but Two is duality, the Self in diremption, in the *double*, no more *esse*, but now *existere*. Counting is nothing in itself; it is a means by which we define relationship, discover order, rhythm and harmony, a means by which we reveal Being. By counting our scale we reveal Being or show Being in relationship, Being revealed. Music is an interpretation of "the music within," the revelation in the soul. If your music is merely counting, however, it is an "empty thing." It must be personal, born of your soul. It must interpret the vibrations or the motions of Being through your soul.

Two means Being in self duplication, viz.: Being *out* of *rest*, in diremption. Being is no more self centered, but exists as the Becoming. An enormous primitive force lies in two; it is intensely personal; with it arises egoity and evil; it means differentiation; the Pythagoreans called it *audacity*. It can express disturbance, but it can also create virtue. Two has been called Patience because we know Patience only by contrast. It has also been called Matter because it is the opposite to One. Two has also been called Nature, because it is the Becoming (from *nascor*, to be born); being the Becoming, it is also the key to One, to Being. Perhaps the most interesting name given to Two, is Love. Two is Love because it is both Being and Becoming; love IS always and BECOMES always.

But One and Two cannot exist apart; they never do. You cannot conceive of Two without a connecting member. Father and Mother invariably unite in the Child. With Unity and Duality is given the Trinity. One and Two belong to one group, are a group for themselves, but their very existence is conditioned by the first member of the following group 3 and 4. Three is called Perfect, for it perfects One and Two; it is called Perfect also because it is the full expression for that which lies Beyond. What is that which lies beyond? It is the esoteric glory of the Divine. The Trinity is the manifested Unity. Three is a divine number like One. Four holds the same relation to Three as Two holds to One in the first group. One represents Being and Two Being in duplication. In the second group, Three represents Being in manifestation and Four represents that manifestation as Human. Four, being Human, was by the Pythagoreans called like man, "the greatest miracle." It is man's figure *par excellence*. It manifests man especially in the Temple, the Square. The square is related to the Trinity as its mother. The Trinity manifests itself in the temple, the square, like One manifests itself in Two.

The third group consists of Five and Six. Again we have the same relationship. Six is related to Five as Four to Three, as Two to One, and, Five, Three and One represent, each in their group, the same idea. Five is "the union of the four elements with Ether," or the square with a dot in the middle, viz.: The Temple with the indwelling Divinity. Five is "the hearty one," *Cordialis*. It unites in friendship the even and the odd, this way:

$$\begin{matrix} 1 & 4 & 7 \\ 2 & 5 & 8 \\ 3 & 6 & 9 \end{matrix}$$

Thus Humanity is united around the Divine. Five is the center of movement between the Universal and the Individual. It is the *at-one-er*, the *creative* hand, that molds existence. It had therefore a phallic character in the ancient religions. Five is really the most interesting number of all and a most extraordinary helpful way for a musician on which to enter the Fourth World, I am talking about in these lectures.

A member: Perhaps, for that reason it is called the Fifth or dominant note.

The lecturer: I must again confess my ignorance of music theory. I did not know that Five is called the dominant note. I have come to this knowledge of the numbers by intuition or by interior revelation, if you like to call it that way. What you say, confirms my words.

Now Six. The Pythagoreans called it "perfection of parts." It is "the marriage number," "the form of forms," "the all sufficient." It is related to Five as Four to Three and Two to One.

You all know Seven as the number of completeness, fullness, perfection. It is the "venerable" number, but related not to divine perfection alone, but also to Human perfection; it is the sevenfold nature of the soul. We are now so far removed from the One, that we have the first of this group, Seven and Eight, no longer a pure type of Unity, it is Union now, union of the Divine and the Human. Hence it is so characteristically called "fullness."

As Four was the human figure, the temple figure, so is its duplication, Eight the same. The Ogdoad is the only "evenly even" number within the Decad. As if referring to the temple, the Greeks said that "all things are eight," and called it Mother.

The last group of the Decad is Nine and Ten. Nine *bounds* all the numbers and Ten denotes the Whole Man. You may continue to twelve, but the plan of grouping must be the same. The first in each group representing something universal, the last something particular, individual.

I am painfully aware of the defectiveness of my presentation. The subject is an immense one and my knowledge so limited because I am not a musician. But I trust to your indulgence. No doubt some of you know more than I do, and I hope that you will study the subject and bring it out in complete form. That the numbers of the scale are so many various *forms or vessels* by which the spiritual content of the musical sounds can be conveyed, I am sure of. Not only shall you be able to enter the Fourth World yourself, by means of this method, but you shall be able to educate your fellow-man in moral and spiritual life in a manner in which education has never been attempted before.

A member: I believe that this is the theory of Wagner, and that all his music was composed accordingly.

The lecturer: Yes, I believe that is one of the secrets of Wagner's influence.

A member: Was he not a mystic?

The lecturer: Yes, he was a mystic. Through Shopenhauer he was connected with the East and there he learned about vibrations and would naturally apply that to his music.

That which I want to convey with this, is not so much something about Vibrations, but I want to have you see everything as Human. Music is the Human, not Mathematics, and I want the Human brought out of it and conveyed to man.

I come to think of Shelley's poem called the Skylark. I wish you to read it. It is indeed untrue to nature. No lark behaves as described by Shelley. But it is not Shelley's purpose to give a nature-description and you feel it, when you have read the poem. You are stirred with the Human, not with Nature. There is a power in this poem similar to St. John's description of the Heavenly Jerusalem. Both authors are not concerned with the description of facts. They are painting pictures with which to convey the Human. Both poems are delineations of character, states, conditions of mind, of that specifically human world, the moral world, or, spiritual world, that world, which man directly creates by manipulating force. It is our world of art, literature, society, history, all that which nature knows nothing of, to which she is blind and indifferent. She even lends herself to be manipulated by man for the upbuilding of his world, but she takes no interest in the work and is as ready to destroy it as to furnish material for it.

We also call that world, the world of freedom, because it is the sphere where man, free from the trammels of an external order, develops his own inner world; where he takes the subject matter out of himself, and the form as well. It is the world by means of which man sees himself outside himself and thus realizes himself, something he could not do but for this world. We of the New Age live in this world.

You may call this Idealism. It is Idealism. As soon as I have seen these lectures in print, I shall write you a book on Idealism, its doctrine and history. Such a book is very much needed for the kernel of all advanced teachings of to-day is idealistic; yet how many know what Idealism really is?

Before I conclude, let us be idealistic for a while. Let me tell you a story, which is thoroughly romantic, but nevertheless the veriest truth.

I say nothing against the various methods proposed by the various teachers, methods by which we are to rise out of ourselves. These methods may be those of the Bhagavad Gita or other Eastern Holy Books; they may be those of the Stoic, the Epicurean, the Christian, etc., they are no doubt excellent methods, *but they are only* methods; in themselves they are nothing. The jewel is in the lotus, but the lotus itself is only a means.

But if you follow the last method of the young girl in this story, I will now tell, you shall have a method, which is not only a method, but which in itself is much more, for it is the life of the Fourth World. The word, that contains all this is *Consecration.* Consecration is not only a Way, but also the Life.

The story is drawn from the Danish philosopher, R. Nielsen, but largely modified by me.

We see a young maiden. A certain stamp of nobility shines on her brow and her bearing is lady-like—still she is only an immature girl. In her present mood she appears dejected. She is a servant in a fine house, but she does not want to be a servant; she feels she is freeborn. She had once begun a course of training designed to give her "a position in life," but now—now that had come to an abrupt end, and she seemed to be far from "a position in life"—she is only a servant, a maid to the lady's maid of the house.

She was goodhearted by nature, kind to the children, and her general deportment was good. She was liked in the house, but nevertheless she was never happy, for she felt *lonesome*—she felt she stood *alone* in the world. She fell into the habit of going to her own room to sit down to cry and to pity herself.

One Sunday afternoon, in one of those odd hours which we all know so well from their intense wearisome nature, she almost broke down. She had just finished a letter to her mother—her poor mother, whom circumstances had brought to the poorhouse. She had not dared to speak about her forlorn life, for she feared to hurt her mother's feelings, and was too good to add to her sufferings. Her own pent up feelings nearly broke her heart. But at last she found relief in the hot tears of agony, and she burst out in prayers for help to understand the meaning of this sorrow.

She did find relief and help. How long she cried she did not know, but all of a sudden she perceived an old man standing at the door. She knew him it seemed. She forgot to ask him how long he had been waiting and what he wanted. Those questions did not seem to be needed, at least they did not suggest themselves. The two engaged in conversation at once, like old friends, knowing each other's affairs. Really they were more than friends. The old man knew all the secrets of the maiden's heart—she had no need of explaining anything to him. He was herself (her Self). Still, upon the direct questions as to why she was weeping, she tried to evade him and could not bring herself at once to a clear statement. But he knew how to talk, and after a little while she confided in him that she wanted to learn (the) Language, Music and Drawing. If she could learn these three arts she could get a "better place" she thought.

"Ah!" said he, "you want to learn (the) Language, Music and Drawing. Very well! You need cry no more; I am an old *pedagogue; I will teach you if you be attentive."

She promised to be attentive! And so the old man began to speak the Language. He spoke the Word: calm, still, intense and affectionate. He spoke and it penetrated to the soul. In his Word she heard all her own thoughts and emotions. Every unclear longing found its expression.

*She learned* (the) Language at once.

"Now, my child," continued the pedagogue, "What is Music?" His expression and intonation were such that she herself could answer the question most readily—the very cords of her heart vibrated and resounded to his question. The question itself contained the answer. The harmony of existence thrilled her through and through. The old friend smiled, raised his finger and said, "This

---
* The highest and most exalted title which the Talmudists bestowed in their most poetical flights upon God himself was that of "Pedagogue of Man."—Em. Deutsch.

is Drawing!" Before her vision the world's idea was revealed. She saw and beheld the ideal forms of life as they passed before her vision. She saw the root and meaning of her own being and the possibilities of all her dreams.

Time passed rapidly away. The midnight hour had come and gone before the guest left her. Before he departed, he admonished her to be silent and preserve her heart pure; to avoid having anything to do with things not pertaining to her life; to be obedient to superiors; and in thought to dwell much upon what he had told her and shown her. He added that if she followed his admonishings she should see him again at some other time.

She made the promise and he departed as suddenly as he had come.

But the young maiden soon fell back to her dreamy and dissatisfied states. The teacher seemed to have taken all that bliss away with him which he brought. She appeared to be more lonesome than ever, and, what was worse, she could not restrain her feelings and ill humor, but became critical and troublesome. She meddled in everybody's affairs and at times refused to obey orders. At last she was called before the lady of the house and reprimanded, and told that she would have to leave the house if she did not change her conduct. She was ordered to her room to think it over all by herself (her Self).

When she came upstairs she found her teacher and friend there awaiting her. The scolding she had received had made her bitter, and she burst out before her friend, upbraiding him as the cause of all her trouble. He had turned her head, the housekeeper had said. If he meant her welfare, he must at once teach her the art of being governess, that she could find another place; this house she would have to leave. If he could not do that he might just as well leave her at once and take all his wisdom with him—it would be of no practical use to her.

"Poor, vain child!" began the pedagogue, the teacher of The Personal, "you have forgotten your promise. It is not my gift that ruins you, it is your unfaithful mind and heart. You have not been obedient and you have angered your superiors. You must repent of that by asking forgiveness from your lady and by changing your conduct entirely. If you do not do that I will leave you, never more to return. Obedience and humility are necessary to learn my wisdom. I shall be sorry to leave you, for then you will be alone indeed!"

The young and pure heart bent down before the kind warning voice. She cried tears such as she never before cried. She begged his forgiveness and that of the lady of the house; she begged everybody to forgive her—and she humbled herself.

Everything now came all right. The pedagogue and best friend came and went. Nobody noticed anything except the radical change that had taken place. Silently and in quiet she gained possession of her soul; and more than once the lady of the house was heard to remark to her husband: "What a sweet soul!"—"Wonderfully gifted!"

Here we might terminate our story. It is of no consequence what became of her afterwards. The main thing is that she is happy and in possession of her soul, and that the old pedagogue takes care of her.

Thus far we have been describing the life of a young girl as represented by the pictures in a book that lies before us. There is still one more picture in the book, and the children declare that it belongs to the story. Evidently the children only look over all the other pictures for the sake of coming to this one, the last of all—but the brightest. It represents a wedding feast, and the bride's features are so much like those of our maiden as we have seen her on the other pictures that we really believe the children. She has been married, and now there is feast in the castle and all the great people of the kingdom are there.

But, where is the teacher? Ah, he sits next to her! He is as happy as she is—perhaps more so! He has been married too.

That has been a soul-marriage indeed! But, if this young being had not been obedient, if she had thought it "too much" to bear the burden of humble submission, there would have been no wedding.

This young girl is an exact copy of thousands in life. Her actions we see daily all around us, her actions up to the time she upbraids the teacher. But we rarely see the *consecrated* woman who follows. Will you follow her example in this last respect?

*Whom have I in the Heavens but Thee; and there is none upon the Earth whom I desire besides Thee.*     *Ps. LXXIII. 25.*

*Lift up your eyes to the Heavens, and look upon the Earth beneath.*
    *Isa. LI. 6.*

*Sing, O ye Heavens, for the Lord hath done it.*
    *Isa. XLIV. 23.*

*Night unto Night showeth knowledge.*     *Ps. XIX. 2.*

*The Moon and the Stars rule by night.*     *Ps. CXXXVI. 9.*

*Even the Night shall be light unto me.*     *Ps. CXXXIX. 11.*

*Arise, let us go by night.*     *Jer. VI. 5.*

*I saw by night.*     *Zech. I. 8.*

# FOURTH LECTURE.

The leading thought in all mythologies is the conflict of Good with Evil, or with the demonic powers. With singular persistency this thought comes to the surface in all legends. The ancients must have had a good reason for this. With some of them this conflict lies in ages past the existence of this universe; with others this conflict is a natural element and law of the present universe. In either case the subject is one of importance.

I have chosen this subject for an introduction to my address on the "Universal Ministry," in which you must serve, because the demonic powers, especially in our day, have gained control where they ought not to have any influence, and it has become your duty to fight them. Among the multitudinous constellations a few stand out very prominently and have by the Chaldeans and Egyptians been called "the signs of the times." If you will look on this sketch of the heavens you readily see these constellations and how they are arranged on both sides of the Milky Way. You can find them very easy in the sky, if you place yourself facing the North star.

Let me say that in the heavens you see, every time you look up, the greatest book of revelations. In indelible ink the figures have been traced there by antiquity—can I say by nature? No scribe can copy them wrongly and no book can be lost. That Bible is inspired indeed; it is written by the hand of God; its word is sacred. Those heavenly scriptures are given for your instruction, and they are profitable for teaching, "that the man of God may be complete."

Around the constellations, I have indicated here merely by their names, you will find on your map a series of demonic powers in the form of dragons and serpents. There are the Northern Dragon, the World serpent and the Hydra; they represent, according to the most ancient traditions, the demonic powers in existence. From all sides they surround and try to crush the universe. While the ancients so forcibly taught this lesson, they also acknowledged that these very powers represented the mystical powers of support. The apparent contradiction is easily solved: The demonic powers were cosmic forces of an earlier existence, either "fallen from their estate" or dethroned for some other reason. Whether fallen or dethroned, they remain cosmic forces, though no longer beneficent forces, but now more or less malignant, not perhaps malignant by nature, but

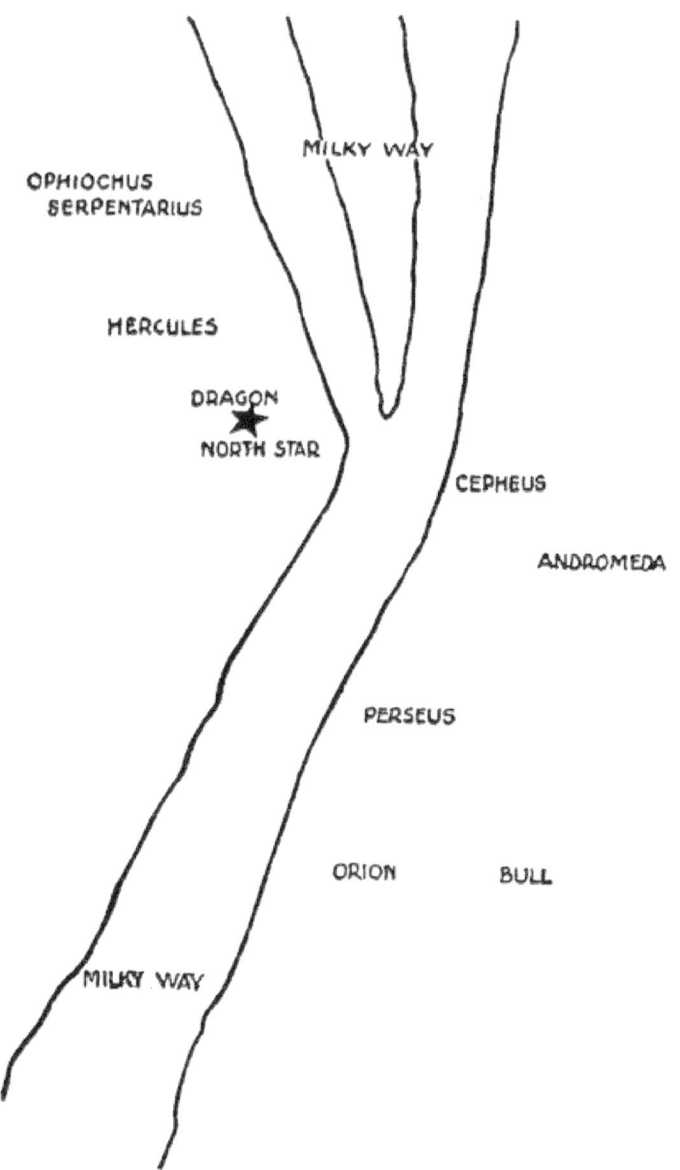

*antagonistic* because progressive eons left them behind. As it was in those days so it is now. The forces we contend against are antagonistic because they are not in order, or line, with the present progress. In the following, I understand by the word demonic all antagonistic powers, forces or circumstances, be they represented by man or not.

To the constellations of the Dragon, Serpent and Hydra come by natural characteristics Scorpio, and Sagittarius, who aims at the heel of Ophiochus. In connection with Scorpio we see the Wolf, the Centaur, Cerberus and the overthrown Altar. Everywhere in the heavens we see conflict. The central figure is Ophiochus in the southern Summer sky. He is the World-spirit in ONE figure, but the gradual development of the World-spirit is represented in THREE figures leading up to him. The three are Orion, Perseus and Hercules.

Orion is the most glorious of the constellations on the Northern winter sky. You all know him, the valiant hero, fighting the raging Taurus, followed by Cetus, the sea monster. He is accompanied by two dogs, symbols of faithfulness; Sirius, the brightest fixed star, in front. Orion is not the biggest, but the best known among the star heroes. When he sets, Ophiochus, the "greatest among the greatest," rises. Orion occupies the same position as Odin accompanied by Thor occupies among the Asas. Both represent the light-world, the cosmic manifestation of the Eternal Intelligence.

Orion was a son of Neptune and a giant and a mightly hunter, and therefore in favor with Diana, who loved him. Her brother, Apollo, was displeased at this and often chid her, to no purpose, however. One day Apollo observed Orion wading through a lake with his head only above water. He called Diana's attention to the black object and declared she could not hit it. Diana aimed and killed Orion. Bewailing her fatal error with many tears she placed him among the stars, where he now follows the chase across the heavens. Sirius follows him and the Pleiades fly before him. At dawn he sinks toward the waters of his father Neptune, but through the winter night he is the giant of the heavens, who fights Taurus, the ferocious Surtur of Norse Mythology or uncontrolled fire, natural necessity.

Orion is human intelligence who fights unrestrained passions, the blind nature powers, the wild and ferocious demonic forces. By intelligence these are controlled—during the hours of night. When day arises with the heavenly orb, the Sun, human intelligence pales and sinks into the sea of the infinite. When summer rules, the "greatest of the great," the Serpent-bearer or Serpent-destroyer, rules the northern heavens and Orion is then visible only in the southern hemisphere. In our present day conflict, human intelligence is the hero that subdues the unruly demonic passions.

When the New Day comes, human intelligence will take a secondary position and the Solar Hero, the Great God, will rule.

Perseus claims our attention next.

When our eye rises from the sinking Orion, we see the beautiful Capella, a star of first magnitude, which never goes entirely below the horizon. It shines in Auriga. Right over it we see Perseus and Andromeda.

You know the myth. Andromeda has been sacrificed, like so many women are, to appease a monster who ravaged her father Orpheus's country. Perseus, the Gorgon-slayer, saw her chained to the rock of sacrifice and sought to find the reason of her disgrace. At first her modesty kept her silent, but finally he learned the true cause. He killed the monster and married Andromeda. In the northern sky, the sea-monster is the northern fish in the zodiac. Cepheus and Cassiopeia, her mother, are seen right above Perseus. The chained princess is the Beauty of the World bound in unfreedom and by grossness. Eternal reason under the form of the imaginative art-impulse liberates the beauty. The true poet and artist is the one who liberates the chained heavenly beauty by descending to the confines of night and in the depths of the soul slays those passion-monsters who hold possession at the springs of life, and who rise from the abyssal sea claiming the daughters of men as their legitimate prey. The true minister is he who bears the armor of truth and beauty and who "in stern tranquillity of wrath" awaits the monster and fearlessly plunges his sword of righteousness into it.

There is no more wonderful picture in the heavens than that of the chained Andromeda. In that myth the ancients represented the very riddle of existence: Why is man chained to this existence? Why the dissonance? Why does every age show so much evil and why must we from time to time rise Perseus-like to liberate our better nature? You, too, must go out to kill the monster, that monster, who in our day threatens the life of our daughter Andromeda, the truly Human. That is the ministry I send you to. You cannot serve your ministry in your own strength, you need the Pegasus, the head of Medusa, and the training of Perseus. When you kill the monster you will hear the cry, "the great Pan is dead."

In Hercules we recognize the giant will, the third psychological form of divine manifestation, also one of the heavenly heroes and champions of freedom. Earthly Hercules is brutal force, unrefined and coarse, almost self-destructive, but the celestial Hercules is moral will, purified endeavor. Like Orion and Perseus, he is one of the greatest heroes in the World-conflict, but unlike these two he is a tragic hero. Though he stands upon the head of the dragon, he nevertheless falls, overcome by his own strength. The falling hero turns in his fall his head toward Ophiochus and learns, like Balder on the funeral pyre, that he shall rise though he falls. Our will only conquers when it ceases to be OUR will. In your ministry you must not go forth in your own strength, but must let the warrior in you do the fighting.

In these three World groups, Orion, Perseus and Hercules, we have the Platonic trinity of the true, the beautiful and the good. Marvelous and beautiful as they are in their significance, they are nevertheless defective. They are earthbound forces and ideas. Neither the true, the beautiful, nor the good can *liberate* man. Neither art nor philosophy brings us *freedom*. And the ancient world knew it.

In Ophiochus antiquity has expressed its deepest insight; has shown that the Divine is incarnated and holds the serpent-demon in its hand, ready to strangle him when the time comes.

Like the Divine, the constellation Ophiochus is so large that but few see it. The Equator goes through the Serpent-bearer's breast and the lower half of his body is never seen on the northern hemisphere; so only half of the Divine is visible to either of the hemispheres, the upper or the lower, the open and the occult. The Greek saw in Ophiochus the great healer and savior, Esculapius, and rightly. Men's dividing lines pierce the breast of Love. The physician comes without arms, trusting to his righteous cause. Ophiochus has no weapons; he steps upon Scorpio and takes no notice of Cerberus; still he grapples with the great Serpent and with his hand alone controls it. Relying solely upon his inherent divinity and superior virtue he stands erect in the conflict, he looks boldly forward to the End of the Age, to Spica, the ripened corn in the hand of the virgin Seraph, the celestial Astrea, and toward the love world of the Twins.

I want you to study carefully and often this great picture-book open in the heavens. It is the Bible which contains the laws, the promises and the prophecies of the Universal Ministry.

I see one form of modern occultism which is lawlessness, and a very dangerous one at that.

We hear of organizations being formed, here and abroad, who stand in with each other and who coöperate to influence the course of history. What right have they to do so? Are they Providence? Are they the executives of the Great Being? Who appointed them? How do they know that they are in possession of the truth and that they influence humanity in the really good? How dangerous is not such a self-appointed Providence? These people are lawless in my opinion. They are seeking their own will; they are anti-Christian, viz., *anti* the spiritual life, which seeks not its own, but inquires from moment to moment what is the Divine Will.

Do not be led astray by these movements. Many societies are now organized in which you involuntarily serve such lawless purposes, if you are a member.

Do not join any secret society. Their day is past. We have no use for them in this nineteenth century, which is the age of democracy, the age of the people. In the past, secret societies were of use when man could not think freely nor be allowed to express himself freely if he had any thought. But we are beyond all that now. There is nothing in the whole range of human knowledge that ought not be public property, if it be beneficent. If it is dangerous it is criminal and ought not to be conveyed even secretly.

You want to work against all these forms of lawlessness.

The most emphatic way you can counteract the modern lawlessness and at the same time a way in which you can come to exert all the secret influence you may desire, consists in entering upon that glorious office to which you and all spiritual people are called, whether brought up on Bible food or not. In quoting the following passage from Peter's letters, I want you to bring it in connection with that which I shall speak of in my next lecture, the excellence of Biblical philosophy.

Peter, speaking to all, called in the Christ principle, to the glory of the great Being, calls them "an elect race, a royal priesthood, a holy nation, a people for God's own possession, that ye may show forth the excellencies of Him, who called you out of darkness into His marvelous light."

You, all of you, called in the Christ principle, are in "that royal priesthood" through which the divine influx comes to the world. In your conversations with God you have realized that. Have you not? Your priesthood is to be made active under the present circumstances of your life, be they at home, in the kitchen, in the shop or before the bar. Your character, such as that is defined by color, is to be made an influence there and at once. No ceremonies are needed. No initiations take place. Arise and look into the Divine Face and you will receive a kiss of love. Let that be the initiation. If you be called from a narrower sphere to a larger, remember it means greater duties and that you are not prepared for the larger sphere, till you have served your apprenticeship at home.

Let the world feel an influence of holiness come to it from your realization of being a "holy nation;" to be holy means to be set apart for special uses!

Let the world understand that you belong to a race, elect to show the excellencies of Him who called you out of darkness. Those who are elected do not mingle with the lawless. How could they return to darkness, which they have just come out of; their election, viz., their growth from out the law, the mean, the unclean protects them. Make sure of your election by study and daily growth, by asserting it, and beware of your lower self, "the dog turning to his own vomits." Increase your treasures, let "the day-star arise in your hearts" by opposing the many false teachers of to-day. They are the false teachers, who by "lascivious doings" promise to reveal mysteries; they are false teachers, who set you up in rebellion against the existing order of things, before you have grown to the New; they are false teachers who tell you that you are a God, forgetting the Human; they are false teachers, who for money and for bank-accounts sell the Divine-Gifts; they are false teachers who only will teach you in secrecy; they are false teachers who teach that which they, themselves, have not lived and experienced; they are false teachers, who substitute an impersonal god for a personal, who gives you an abstract conception for a concrete; what have you gained? False teachers everywhere! False teachers abound!

*Brighu, whose heart was the pure essence of virtue, who proceeded from Manu himself, thus addressed the great sages: "Hear the infallible rules for the fruit of deeds in this universe."*

*Manu Lawbook.*

# FIFTH LECTURE.

I want now to impress upon you the idea of religion as regards your ministry. Of course, you understand that I am not going to speak theology. I shall speak simply about religion as universally understood, and have nothing to do with the dogmas of any special religion.

Religion is consciousness of God and an active love to God. Religion presupposes a distinction between God and the World, God and Man, but is also a relationship of union between the two. Religion is therefore really an expression for man's company with God. Both philosophy and art concern themselves with man's relationship to God; the first expresses that relation in thought; the latter does it in plastic forms or by color, etc. But neither of them represents a life in God. Religion does. Religion is personal living and doing in God. It is this idea I want to emphasize. And this is a new side of that fourth form I spoke of before, and *the* form you must live in, in order to fulfill your ministry religiously; yea, which you must live in, in order to fulfill your ministry perfectly.

Follow that great teacher, whom the world looks to as the Christ. Follow him, viz., do as he did, live as he lived, etc. I am not now laying much emphasis upon his teachings, be they ethical, dogmatic, etc. I point to the religion of Jesus, to the way he had religion. To find what his religion was, or what consciousness he had of his relationship to the Father, look upon the praying Christ, the Christ in retirement on the hills; look to the Jesus of love in that wonderful high-priestly address given us by John, the apostle; imitate the trusting Christ, see that faith, that adores, and give way to that tenderness which wept over Jerusalem. Do that and you shall understand the Religion of Jesus, and you shall get religion; not the religion of the scribes or the doctors, but the religion of the pious heart, the child's simplicity and faith. You shall thus go forth a power and redeem your fellow men. You redeem him from sin when you show him his disobedience, and he asks the Great Being to be forgiven; you redeem him from his ignorance, when you teach him that the A B C of religion is to cry "Father;" you redeem him from his degraded life, when you cause him to bathe, to hope, to smile and to start anew to carve out a life. You become a Redeemer in that way.

All this I have now said is or ought to be acceptable to you, whether you look upon the Lord as a man or as a God.

There is another thing you want for your ministry, and that is more reading in the Bible. Of course you will believe me when I say that I am not a bibliolater and have no by-purposes in recalling you to the Bible. I will not take you away from your Orientalism. No, not for a moment. Study with the Orientals early and late. Invite them to this country in great numbers and learn all they have to teach you. I have heard nothing that is not sound from these men. I know many of them personally; some of them I love; for all I have the greatest respect. But this is a fact, easily enough verified, that historically we are farther on in development than they, for to-day they teach and pride themselves that they teach doctrines many thousand years old. Historical progress means much. It means advancement, it means additions, it means deeper and new experiences, for we with our globe have come, on the spiral movement, to a position in the universe, where other and more factors have come to play than were known thousands of years ago. Another fact, also easily verified, is this, that we as Western people are radically different from those of the East. We have grown out of another soil, and we live differently, and *cannot live as the Orientals* live, even if we wanted to. These and many other differences make it impossible for us to accept many if not most of the details of Eastern teachings. We may learn from them on general subjects, however. We have neither their depth nor their subtlety. We have not their peaceful natures, nor their simplicity; and I wish to God that our American people could learn something on those lines. I say this and I can say much more that is favorable to the Orientals, but they need not my recommendation. You have so many of them right here in Chicago, that you know perfectly well what they are and what they can do.

You understand me now as regards the Oriental Bible. Let me now say a word or two for the Western Bible.

Every one of the most important doctrines, which the Orientals teach you and lay so much stress upon, are found in your much-neglected Bible, and, as a rule, it seems to me, better stated there; at any rate, those doctrines are stated there in a form more suited to our use. Let me review some of the more important ones.

Let me begin with the doctrine of illusion, Mâyâ. Turn to Ecclesiastes or the Preacher and you read: "Vanity of vanities, said the Preacher, Vanity of vanities; the whole is vanity. What advantage is to man by all his labor, etc." That's the philosophy of Ecclesiastes, and exactly, in Hebrew rendering, the doctrine of Mâyâ. We have the same teaching in ordinary church theology. There the doctrine runs: "Forsake the devil, the flesh and the world," and the reason is the same: they are illusory. The undertone of the whole Bible is the same.

We learn that *Sat-Chit-Ananda*—Existence, Knowledge and

Bliss—are the characteristics of Being in manifestation; we learn that Atman, the only true existence, Self, is THAT, which alone endures, while everything else changes and disappears. In the Bible we have a wonderful parallel to this teaching and one more personal or more direct than the philosophy of the East. In Col. I we read that "Christ is the principle in whom all things stand together." In true oriental fashion we have here a person spoken of as a principle, and, moreover, declared to be the principle in "whom all things stand together." What is this but teaching in St. Paul's fashion that the Self is the enduring element? This same Christ is elsewhere declared to be "the way, the truth and the life;" does this trilogy not answer marvelously to Existence, Knowledge and Bliss?

As for that terrible dogma of Karma, we can beat that with the Old Testament teachings about the Law. No man can fulfill the law, and the law is the condemnation of man. Indeed, the Bible holds that that which we sow, we shall reap, and that we are judged by our fruits, and that we are saved by our works, etc.

This dogma of Karma and that of the law is only partially true. Life does show us cases where the uttermost farthing has been asked. Often it seems that we atone for our sins and pay the penalty for every mistake. But as true as it is that nature shows straight lines—lines of righteousness—so true is it also, that she shows curves, lines of love, and it is a fact, that she shows more curves than straight lines. What does this show? It shows that there is an abundance of love and mercy to counterbalance the straight lines, and the demands, which these make because we do not follow them. Have we not individually experienced that there is forgiveness? Ah! there is an ocean of mercy, deep and large enough to swallow up all Karmic influences and Karmic sins! Mankind—excepting the Hindus and the Jews—believes it and its experience is a warrant for its belief. Though we do not know the exact workings of Law and Forgiveness; neither do we know all about Karma. Let us rest assured that there is mercy as well as law. We may even go so far as to take the Christian teaching for our guide and say that so long as we are under the law, we are judged by the law, and when we place ourselves under mercy, we receive mercy.

Some of the Orientals will not admit our dogma of curves, of mercy. I spent the most of a night with Chatterdi Mohini, when he was here, some years ago, discussing the dogma. He would not admit the curves nor mercy, but counted them both as Karma, good Karma. The logical contradiction of a finite man making good Karma strong enough to redeem him, he would not see. Other Orientals are not so rigid. I believe they have learned mildness in the West. The whole doctrine of Karma, it should be remembered, is really a philosophical play toy of latter date. As now taught, or as it has been taught for a thousand years or more, it is not found in the Vedas. The Jewish harsh doctrine of Law is a product of the scribes and scholastic doctors of Egypt. Both Karma and the Law are the clocks of sanctimoniousness. Love is the key to life and mercy makes the world move.

Then there is the great doctrine of Nirvana: union with the Divine, howsoever that be conceived by the various schools. Jesus has declared: "The Father and I are one," and that is true for every man. We always were in Nirvana, and when our Mediæval Mystics speak of Union with God, they mean to reassert this fundamental doctrine of the West and remind themselves and their hearers of it. Our Bible ends with the declaration that God shall be all in all, and it opens with the picture of God creating man in his own image. Between these two, the End and the Beginning, every page teaches how this nirvanic bliss was forgotten and how it is recovered. And the Bible is not uncertain in its teachings nor indefinite in its definition of Nirvana. Nowhere does it teach a loss of The Personal, or the Essential in Man, the most irrational of all Eastern teachings. The Bible teaches that we *find ourselves* in God. That "flaming glory," the soul, which left the Deity on that morning of creation, does not return empty to its source. It returns heavily laden with experience. It is "the Divine in Diremption," and returns to itself plus its human experience. Souls have been returning ever since "the divine awakened in man," and the DIVINE IS BECOMING HUMAN. It is therefore that I say so often in these lectures and addresses that EVERYTHING IS HUMAN. I proclaim a great Mystery! Thus it is! THE DIVINE IS HUMAN.

The cry is for Adeptship. Mahatmas are wanted everywhere. Let the world have them, but why necessarily go to India to become an adept by those peculiar ascetic methods, there adopted, especially as the adept produced is a recluse and one who shuns human society? Why not fulfill the law implied in the Sermon on the Mount. He is an Adept, a Mahatma, a Great Spirit, who lives up to that sermon; and that sermon does not drive you into selfish seclusion to give you powers outside human uses and society. The Sermon on the Mount is eminently practical. We need that sort of adeptship. One who possesses those eight Blessings has certainly attained the Universal Consciousness so much desired, but rarely tried for among the modern aspirants for mahatmaship. The truth is that most of the candidates condemn themselves by their methods. External methods are for the materialistic; the method of the Sermon on the Mount is purely spiritual. Everyone seeks his methods according to his disposition.

The moderns talk a great deal about *overcoming*, so much so that the talk has become Cant. Of course, we must learn to overcome, and the first step in overcoming self is to keep still about our work of overcoming. Overcoming is proved by overcoming: "The truth shall make you free." We are judged not by works, but by our fruits, and spiritual fruits cannot be seen by the vulgar.

The Hindus offer us many kinds of Yogas or means of overcoming. They are all fine and we have them all in our Bible, and under forms more suited to our wants. There is Karma Yoga, the yoga of work, which teaches that by incessant and faithful work you will liberate yourself from all kinds of bondage, attain supreme wisdom and finally lapse into the Deity. This is magnificent philosophy, true to the uttermost, but there is more in religion than there is in philosophy. He, whose *work* consists in *giving* himself, that others may live, and who gives himself after God's own example—God is both sacrificer, the sacrifice and the sacrificial lamb—he is a pattern for others to follow and unites in his character both religion and philosophy. Turn to your New Testament and you will see two such workers in Peter and James. Read their epistles.

The Bhakti Yoga, the yoga of love, is beautifully illustrated in John and his gospel, "The Heart of Christ." I have already spoken of the Sermon on the Mount; it is all Bhakti Yoga. Our mediæval mysticism is full of this yoga. Holy Graël and Romanticism are Bhakti Yoga.

Gnana Yoga holds that man is essentially divine. I have spoken of that already. By the Gnana Yoga we are to attain freedom, to go beyond this or that form of existence and to stand in Being. Is not this fully declared in the apostle's word: "Not I, but Christ in me?" How rich is not this word and how practical! Here is a personal power, we can imitate, no abstraction. Here is religion, not merely philosophy.

Raja Yoga, the psychological yoga, recommends concentration as a means of union with God. If you will look through, once more, the lectures I delivered here in the Spring, you will see how elaborate Mysticism is on this subject, and the Mysticism I defined is all an outgrowth of the Bible.

All these Yogas blend most beautifully in the true Christian religion. And our Western view has an advantage over the Oriental. By the Yogas of India we are led to an *impersonal God*, to an undifferentiated God, but do we gain anything by that? Why and how is an oriental impersonal God better than the Western theological and personal God? They are both of no use to the spiritual man! We want no dogmatic God of any kind! We want the *whole* God, the *whole* man! *We want fullness!* I claim we get that sooner by means of the Bible than by the Yogas.

Not only has the Bible shown itself the superior, when we

compare it to the most universal teachings of India, but intrinsically it has claims upon our attention and study.

For you, who are to engage in the Universal Ministry in these days, it is important that you should have a definite program to offer, and a program which is not only essentially biblical, but which also contains the essence of the Bible.

Please look at this diagram:

| | | | |
|---|---|---|---|
| Right Belief | 1. I am the Lord, thy God, etc. | 1. Our Father who art in Heaven, Hallowed be Thy name. | 1. Blessed are the poor in spirit, for theirs is the kingdom of Heaven. |
| Right Thought | 2. Thou shalt not take the name of the Lord thy God in vain. | 2. Hallowed be Thy name. | 2. Blessed are they that mourn, for they shall be comforted. |
| Right Speech | 3. Keep the Sabbath day holy. | 3. Thy kingdom come. | 3. Blessed are the meek, for they shall inherit the earth. |
| | 4. Honor thy father and thy mother, etc. | 4. Thy will be done on earth as it is in Heaven. | 4. Blessed are they that hunger and thirst after righteousness, for they shall be filled. |
| Right means of livelihood | 5. Thou shalt not kill. | 5. Give us this day our daily bread. | 5. Blessed are the merciful, for they shall obtain mercy. |
| Right endeavor | 6. Thou shalt not commit adultery. | 6. Forgive us our trespasses, etc. | 6. Blessed are the pure in heart, for they shall see God. |
| Right memory | 7. Thou shalt not steal. | 7. May we not fall into temptation. | 7. Blessed are the peacemakers, for they shall be called sons of God. |
| Right meditation | 8. Thou shalt not bear false witness against thy neighbor. | 8. Deliver us from evil. | 8. Blessed are they that have been persecuted for righteousness' sake, for theirs is the kingdom of Heaven. |
| | 9. Thou shalt not covet thy neighbor's wife. | 9. Thine is the kingdom, etc. | 9. Blessed are ye when men shall reproach you, and persecute you, and say all manner of evil |
| | 10. Thou shalt not covet thy neighbor's house, etc. | | 10. Against you falsely, for my sake. Rejoice, etc. |

I have arranged the Decalogue, the Lord's Prayer, and the Beatitudes in parallel columns, and for completeness I have added the Buddhistic "law," if I may so call it, the nearest I can find, that corresponds to the balance of the program. Indeed, the East seems singularly barren just here.

My object has been to demonstrate not only the inner connection between the Decalogue, the Lord's Prayer and the Beatitudes, but to show you what and how to do.

Let me explain the diagram.

The Decalogue has a very great interest for us, and is binding, not because it is the will of an arbitrary lawgiver, be he divine or human, but because it expresses our innermost nature. The law is the law of human conduct. Only by being obedient to it can we live right. It is a transcript of our moral necessities. The Decalogue is universal, not national. Let us see how it expresses human nature.

That which we are commanded to do or not to do in the Decalogue, we pray for or against in the Lord's Prayer, viz., we sigh for it.

> "Prayer is the soul's sincere desire,
> Unuttered or unexpressed;
> The motion of a hidden fire,
> That trembles in the breast.
>
> Prayer is the burthen of a sigh,
> The falling of a tear,
> The upward glancing of an eye
> When none but God is near."

When we pray, we of the New Age, we pray not as those of ancient days, who implored or petitioned an absent or angry God. Such an attitude implies a fall;

> "................addressing Thee
> We sin, because we separate ourselves
> In thought from Thee who art our very self;
> For we are nothing if we are not 'Thou,'
> And Thou art 'we;'     *     *     *"

We sigh or express ourselves, when we pray, that our life may be perfect, that He may awaken to self-consciousness of His existence in our heart. We sigh that our true self expressed in ethical forms in the Decalogue may be realized; and our sigh is expressed in those prayers standing opposite to the "laws."

The plenitude of the moral law of the Decalogue and our sigh of the Lord's Prayer is expressed in the Blessings put in the corresponding column and paragraphs. What are these blessings but the fulfillment of our struggles? They are indeed the crowned life!

What new life this comparative view brings out before us! How rich our religious heritage is; how colossal the moral life rises in its simplicity! How attractive everything becomes! Is the spirit of these laws and sayings not full of inspiration? How easy it is now to work in one's ministry to man!

Let me now point out the details.

The first law is the declaration that Being is our Lord. "Self is the lord of self, who else could be the lord," is the way it is put in the Dhammapada. This is bed rock. We recognize this by giving utterance to it in the first prayer: "Our father, who art in heaven," and our prayer is lifted out of the mere philosophic cognition and becomes a warm uplift of heart. This heart transformation of a cold intellectual truth is a result of "poverty of spirit," viz., that singleness of mind, which sees the Father everywhere. "Poverty of spirit" is itself a gift, a Blessing, and contains in it the assurance of the kingdom of heaven. Who can tell which of the three is first, and which is last? Neither is first, nor last nor middle. They are three in one, each other's father, mother, child. Who will doubt that here we have the "Right Belief?"

It is easy to see that our natural law is "not to take the Lord's name in vain." It follows as a natural corollary from the former. Equally natural it is that we should sigh "hallowed be thy name." This is so natural that we wonder how it is possible for "the world" to be profane and to be false to its great call; yet "the world" is "fallen" and we mourn and cry over Jerusalem. Those of the kingdom and those in training for the kingdom are happy at the bottom of their hearts, but in "the world" they mourn and have no happiness; there can be none for them. But though they mourn, they shall be comforted sometime, for "the world" cannot prevail; they carry their blessings with them, not only in the power they exert themselves by hallowing the Name, but as a direct gift, for in their sigh lies a fulfillment of their innermost desire: the Lord's glorification. Is this not Right Thought?

"Keep the Sabbath day holy." What is the Sabbath day in our constitution? When do we have Sabbath according to the natural law of our being? When we are at Rest and Rest means a higher harmony, a universal peace and consciousness of the Allpresence. Ought we not keep that holy? What is it to keep it holy? It means setting it apart for special spiritual and ideal purposes. When in ecstasy, we ought not to defile the Divine by dragging it in the mire. How natural that we pray "Thy kingdom come." What is the kingdom but a societary enlargement of the subjective Sabbath? Who can attain the Sabbath Rest? Those mighty ones, who in their own powers rule the states—for a while? Nay! The meek shall inherit that kingdom the Lord purposed from Eternity, for they are the ones who already have it in them.

With these three parallels closes the first division of the Decalogue, the Lord's Prayer and the Blessings. They relate to the Divinity. The next division, the fourth parallel, is small but rich. As the first expresses the Divine, so does the second express the Human, the Human in fullness. That which in the first is Being, is in the second the Becoming. And obedience to the second division proves obedience or fulfillment of the first.

"Honor thy father and mother," etc. Is not this the foundation-thought of all human life in society? Take away the father and mother idea and we are in the sphere of the beast. What becomes of our distinctive human life, our arts, sciences and society if reverence be removed? They are no more! They are built upon a "ground, we do not tread upon;" upon an idea, purely human. As Being is the *sine qua non* universally, so Honor is the *sine qua non* in morals.

You have heard that the Jews attributed a life to the Decalogue. They considered it a living being. How profound! How significant, that the parallel prayer to this commandment is the sigh that "Thy will be done on earth as it is in heaven," or as some will have it "Thy fixed purposes in heaven and earth." The Lord's will is the establishment of the Human, the Temple built in the form of a man, His Own Manifestation. Father and Mother are the symbols of that temple. Let me show you this by defining the nature of a symbol. When you look deep enough you will find that you cannot utter a single sentence without speaking in symbols. Language, thoughts, sentiments, emotions are but symbols or echoes. The reason is this, that Nature, as she lies diffused around us, is immortal language, though latent: the language of that Great Being whose image we find stamped upon our own souls. Wherever we look—toward the infinitely Great or toward the infinitely Small—we see harmonies of mind and nature, and each such harmony is a symbol. Wherever we listen, we hear the tunes that announce the perpetual and unceasing incarnation of the Great All in the works of creation. And what is a tune but a symbol? A symbol of the esoteric glory of the Deity.

Wherever we discover an avenue or path that leads to God, we step upon an emblem, and a symbol stares us in the face.

No flower blows for its own sake; its brilliant colors reveal the sweetness of The Beloved; its perfume IS the love of The Beloved.

The brilliant plumes of tropical birds reflect the golden lights of the Heavenly City.

When mountains call to mountains, we hear in the echo, the answer from The Beloved, that He will come soon.

In the bark of the dog, the lowing of cattle and the roar of the wild beast, you hear that longing for home, which is so universal throughout creation.

The sun rises but to assure us of the greater day of eternity, which is coming; and sets in the evening upon the ocean to show us the "golden bridge" to heaven.

This is not fancy nor extravagant language, but sober truth.

It is evident then that a symbol is no arbitrary figure. It is (1) an harmony of mind and nature; it is (2) a tune that announces the incarnation of the Deity. I may also, using the words of Wordsworth, say, that in symbols I

.......... oftentimes
Hear the still, sad music of humanity.

Why did Wordsworth say the *sad* music of humanity? Why do I repeat the word?

Here is a story that may explain it. It is attributed to Attar, the Persian Sufi poet. A thirsty traveler dipped his hand into a spring of water to drink from the hollow hand as from a cup. Another traveler came likewise to drink, but he drank from an earthen bowl and left it behind him. The first traveler used it for another drink and was surprised to find the same water bitter when drank from the earthen cup. But a voice from heaven told him that the clay from which the bowl was made was once Man, and, into whatever shape renewed, can never lose the bitter flavor of mortality. So it is. The gift of humanity is a bitter-sweet drink. It is music, but *sad* music. Humanity is much like a splendid ruin. It is as much a veil as a revelation. And so all our symbols are living beings, Undines, to whom we have given our souls. In them we see reflected the greatest splendor: the divine in man, but we see also the frail and weak sensuous man, who stands in his own light. He was once, according to the legend, the temple in which abode the Holy Graël. But the Holy Graël was taken away and is now in the air, hovering over him, awaiting another Titurel to rebuild the temple. And so by

The sad music of humanity

is symbolized the past splendor, when the Holy Graël was still present, and the present sorrow, that the Holy Graël has been taken away.

I speak of symbols as expressions of these three great forms of life: (1) as harmonies of Mind and Nature; (2) as tunes that announce the incarnation of Deity; and (3) as the music of humanity. The first form covers all our philosophy; the second all our religion, and the third all our art and science.

But—is there no relation between Symbols and Home? Indeed there is!

That harmony between Mind and Nature, which I have called a symbol, and which I just said was the sphere of our philosophy—that harmony is only realized in the true home.

That tune from above, the perpetual incarnation of the Divine in the works of creation, which I also called a symbol and which I just said was the sphere of our religion—that incarnation of divine life is realized only in the true home.

That "sad music of humanity," which all deeper souls hear in symbols and which all noble hearts feel throughout all works of art, be they of nature or man, that "sad music of humanity," the bitter-sweet gift of the gods—marriage—is realized only in the true home.

The true home, then, is the most COMPREHENSIVE SYMBOL. On one side it is Mind and on the other it is Nature. On one side it is divine and on the other it is human. Home is the *actuality* of all desire, thought, love and aspiration. Philosophy, Religion and Art are *im*personal and idealistic. Home contains them all, and is far more, for Home on the *human plane* answers to that which *Theology* calls the trinity. Home is a realization of that most marvelous relationship of Father—Son—Spirit. It *actualizes* this trinity in the mystery of union between Father—mother—child.

Again, Home on the human plane means that which Nature so vainly tries to symbolize. It means *incarnation*.

Nature is a "system of nuptials," a perpetual bearing, a Becoming, a bringing forth, but *her child is blind*. The stone sleeps, the trees rise toward the sun—but great care is taken, as Goethe remarked, that they do not grow into heaven. The animal moves, but moves hither and thither and knows not why. But man opens his eyes and can say "I"—the very appellative of the Divine. Man can rise and grow into heaven, because he came from heaven, a "trailing cloud of glory." Man can move with freedom and build a world for himself, can erect himself as a temple for the Divine, and that temple is Home.

In one word Home is the term, the full, comprehensive expression for all this! That's home! That's the relationship of home and symbology.

I speak, then, of symbols as expressions of these four forms of life: (1) as harmonies of Mind and Nature; (2) as tunes that announce the perpetual incarnation of Deity; (3) as the music of humanity; and (4) as expressions of that most wonderful temple of all temples, which man has erected or can erect: Home.

Do you begin to see why we should honor father and mother? By way of the Home you do!

There are still other characteristics of Home, I must mention here, for they reveal the spiritual meaning of the fourth commandment. The baking of bread is one of the main symbols of a home. There is no home where bread is not baked. The rudiments of civilization and home life are first found when breadbaking begins. Those peoples who live simply of fruit have not yet settled and come under the forms of civilization. No family hearth exists among them. The hearth is the family altar, the earliest rudiments of home, the first moral factor. The deeper signification of bread is wonderful and amazing. In bread we eat indeed, as Paracelsus said, heaven and earth, for they have both worked to make it. Bread is thus literally "the principle in which all things stand together," a phrase St. Paul uses about the Christ. And what is that principle but love. In all mythologies bread does signify love. Again, in bread we *eat* the father and mother principle; father is heaven, mother is earth. So it is in all mythologies.

It will now be seen how profound is the relationship between the fourth commandment and the prayer that parallels it. It will also readily be seen why the Blessing connected with this commandment and this prayer is expressed in forms of "hunger and thirst." The three thoughts are expressed in symbols of generation and regeneration, the most profound mysteries of life, all, however, meaning the Human! How weak the Buddhistic "Right Speech" is, compared to all this Western Bible symbolism! I do not know that any Buddhistic school, not even a Northern one, has put so much into the third *anga* of the "noble eightfold Path."

The fifth commandment is. "Thou shalt not kill." It is the first of the third division. In this division all the commandments are negative and the prayers are against the evils implied in the commandments.

We kill by every antagonistic thought, mien, act or word; by everything which destroys the kingdom of peace and love, the Lord purposed from the Beginning. We pray for the opposite virtue when we ask for the daily bread, for bread is, as I said before, Love. In the corresponding beatitude we are assured that mercy shall bring mercy. The following five commandments seem contained in this, the fifth. The Buddhistic "Right means of livelihood" may imply that our living (in the widest sense) is not by killing or taking, but by gifts.

Adultery is any and all kinds of falsifications. We are constantly committing adultery, hence we constantly pray for forgiveness. We know from the Bible and from Mythology, that none shall see God and live; hence we must conclude that the purity here required must be of an angelic order. We understand why none shall see God and live; we are all adulterers or falsifiers. The Buddhist wisely limits his demands on this point to an endeavor: Right Endeavor.

"Thou shalt not steal." Who has never stolen? Who can say that he or she will not do it again? None can say it truly, for we break this commandment seventy times a day. Our pride steals God's honor; our dishonest or imperfect thoughts steal Universals which we attribute to ourselves; we steal the very air we breathe if we do not accept it as a gift, a blessing; we steal our neighbor's good name, etc. as well as his goods. We are thieves and robbers from mother's womb to our graves. We need, indeed, to pray that we fall not into temptations and a very high prize is set for those who make peace on earth, those who try not to steal or make a disturbance in God's order. Indeed, they are worthy to be called "sons of God," for they work on behalf of the kingdom. The Buddhistic parallel to this, the seventh commandment and seventh prayer, is so abstract and far off as to have no bearing upon the subject before us. It is certainly Right Memory to remember the law against stealing, but memory does not free us from temptation.

We hear further repetitions of these last mentioned commandments in the eighth against bearing false witness, and the eighth prayer is an emphatic cry for deliverance. The Blessing for those who have not borne false witness and therefore have been persecuted is the highest gift: the Kingdom of Heaven. Logically we could expect nothing less; they are simply entitled to that kingdom, for they have made it by their uprightness.

In the ninth and tenth commandments we come to ultimates, the vulgar violence of coveting. The spiritually minded does not even pray against this vice. It is impossible that he or she could covet. Instead of praying they sing the doxology and rejoice in their Blessing.

I have now given a rapid survey of these wonderful teachings of the Bible and leave it to yourself to judge whether I am right or not in the assertions I made in the beginning of this lecture. I claim to be right.

And now, in conclusion, I want you to organize in order to carry out some one line of these parallels. Take any one of them. Stick to it and you shall find that by fulfilling any one of them, you fulfill them all. Come together and sign a pledge, that you to the best of your ability will fulfill, say, the fifth law, fifth prayer, and get the fifth Blessing.

I will stop for a moment here and ask Miss Farmer to speak on the Universal Ministry, because she has set it up at Greenacre, and Greenacre is no more an experiment, but very largely, as you all know, or ought to know, a realization of the ideas I have set forth on the Universal Ministry.

Miss Farmer: I feel it is a great privilege to stand beside

Prof. Bjerregaard and bear witness to the wonderful help he gave to us at Greenacre in realizing our ideal. The little work which you hear spoken of by the name of Greenacre originated because a few of us got a glimpse of what it is to be a son and daughter of God—to be in this world to manifest the wonderful power of God to the world.

The sacredness of it and the beauty of this ministry came with great power upon us; and we realized that throughout the world, in every corner of the world, were devoted sons and daughters living the life of purity and consecration; we felt the power of those who had gone before us, and we felt the power of those who were working in distant places, in mountain fastnesses and desert places, and it seemed to us that it would be a great benefit and strength to us all, if we could, in our little corner, call together those devoted ones, to confer about the wonderful kingdom of God. We called them together. That gathering is Greenacre. Men say to us sometimes, we don't want to talk about those things; we are here to live a common life, to pay attention to things that are practical. But some of us feel that the kingdom of God is the one thing in the world that is practical; and it was to show its practicability and its fitness to every condition of life that a few of us went to the banks of that beautiful river between Maine and New Hampshire, the Piscataqua, and sat down there in quietness, and invited the loftiest souls to come and tell us about their work and show how it was related to the kingdom of God. We realized that there was nothing in the world, without some good in it, nothing in which God may not manifest himself and speak his Word. It was said to us in the beginning when we called to us the highest we could find in art, "what has art to do with religion?" We felt that it had everything to do with religion; that art was the broad avenue by which many souls would come to their father; we had art lectures to help people to realize that art was an avenue, a ministry, almost as sacred—art has many forms—or more sacred than anything else. We felt this, too, that of all the privileges that are given to the world to-day, all the problems that are agitating us, that are being pondered upon day and night, every question could be answered before the sun set, if every soul in the world had found the kingdom of God in its own soul, had found harmony and peace and were trying to bring it into the world. As soon as we find that harmony we become a law in ourselves.

In looking for an emblem, we wanted something that would be a call to everybody and fit everybody, and we felt that the message that had been brought to the world by prophet after prophet, was the message of peace. We realized that that was the one thing the world needed more than all else. People are seeking happiness and joy in every avenue. So we put a large banner over our heads with these letters on it, PEACE, and we asked every child of God who came to us to give us the fullest message, the largest word which he had to say or to bring, but with no word of criticism, nothing about the other brother's way of working. We felt it was a great privilege to have representatives from the East in that opening summer; to feel that we were clasping hands as brothers and that the cord we were stretching would extend around the world. At first it was only a little work, but it has been such a blessing; it has been so to many, and there are those in this room who can testify to the blessings that have come to them. I think there ought to be such a consecrated spot in every part of our country—all cannot come to Greenacre, it is only a little place—but everybody can form a little Greenacre in his own life and with others. People ask what Greenacre is, if it is this thing or that or the other. I say it is Greenacre. I cannot define it. The moment we define we limit. It has been the spirit of God working in our midst; it has been perfect freedom. We expected money to help us forward, but that door was closed and we seemed called to go forward without money. Then the word came with strong force, "Not by might or power but by my Spirit, saith the Lord," and we felt strongly that there was a power beyond money on which we could depend. THERE IS A POWER THAT COMES FROM RIGHTEOUSNESS. We thought if we had money we saw things that could be done, but we found they could be done without money. This became our trust. We found it was God's work; all the money we needed came just as we needed it, just at the right time, because God would move some heart, who recognized its stewardship, to help us. Dear friends, it is one of our joys that we are just as necessary to God as God is to us.

It seems to me this afternoon, when I thought over of all the beautiful messages, that have come to us there, which of all I should lay you most to heart, that would mean the most to you, that it was meekness. Meekness is the greatest force in life. The victories of the world are won by the meek. Prof. Bjerregaard has said to us, that we must submit, and so it is, we submit in cheerfulness and gladness, because we have found that to be the way, that leads to God. Of all things, when we can conquer the personal self and let the power of God work through us, then we may safely go forward without any fear of anything. There can then be no lack; no good thing shall be withheld. That has been the dominant spirit at Greenacre.

There has been no personal leadership. Every soul that came there felt that it was his own work as much as it was anybody else's, and did it. Each one sunk his personal self in the common good, and found that the one joy was service, service for service's sake, love for love's sake.

Think of the tired, anxious workers in business here in this city; many of them working to fulfill God's work in the world, with anxious thoughts, not knowing what will happen six months hence. If they could see this wonderful law of trust and meekness, no failure could come to them. We are endeavoring to bring it into the business world.

I could name many great souls here in Chicago, who have strengthened us in our needs, and we believe that Greenacre is just as much the work of Chicago as it is the work of the East, and it belongs just as much to the Orient as to the Western lands. The words that have been spoken there from the Orient have been words of life to many souls. I think that in time to come there will be many Greenacres all over the world dedicated to God and testifying to the truth of the vision. None has seen it more clearly than the teacher who stands before us to-day. None has held us to a higher ideal than he does. You know of the Crusaders who went forth searching for the Holy Graël, which was supposed to be the cup in which the blood of the Savior was held. There is now a new crusade inaugurated, not to search for the Holy Graël, for it was found, but to go forth in this new ministry—to go forth like the knights of old. How did those knights of Mount Salvate live? They must live lives, pure in thought and word and deed. The spirit was upon them and they went forth with knowledge,—they knew where wrongs were to be redressed and they went forth and redressed the wrongs; but they could never speak of their works. If they did they must come back. And this law of silence is one of the greatest to learn, but you must learn it. You must not speak of yourself as a Knight of Mount Salvate. Most of us are like the young convert, so full in the beginning. When he got the first glimpses, he felt he must tell everybody; but in many cases he forged darts which came back upon him, because of imprudences. It is now perhaps eight or ten years ago, when a clergyman in the West sent me a letter in which he said, that the true indispensable of spiritual work was silence and struggle, silence lest the divine atoms should be dissipated in speech, and struggle because the natural man rejects the divine man. I thought once I had learned what struggle was, but silence was so hard. I found as I got on in my experience, that the secret of power lies in silence.

The lecturer: Let Greenacre be an encouragement to you. The Universal Ministry has been set up there in one form. Greenacre is no experiment, but is a reality; so real, that it can be imitated. Will you not follow the example here in the neighborhood of Chicago? I will help you, Miss Farmer will help you.

*This so solid-seeming world, after all, is but an air-image over Me, the only reality; and Nature, with its thousand-fold production and destruction, but the reflex of our own inward force.—*
*T. Carlyle.*

*We see the world piece by piece, as the sun, the moon, the animal, the tree; but the whole, of which these are the shining parts, is the soul. From within or from behind a light shines through us upon things, and makes us aware that we are nothing, but the light is all.*
*R. W. Emerson.*

# SIXTH LECTURE.

### INVOCATION.

Ye deities! who fields and plains protect,
Who rule the seasons, and the year direct,
Ye fauns—
Ye nymphs that haunt the mountains and the plains
\* \* \* \* \* bring
Your needful succor. \* . \* \* \* \*
Leave, for a while, O Pan! thy loved abode,
You who supply the ground with seeds of grain,
And you, who swell those seeds with kindly rain,
Be ye propitious \* \* \* \* \*
\* \* \* \* hear and grant our prayers.
(Comp. Georgics I, 1-64.)

This evening we come to a new subject. I shall speak no more on Soul-Development and shall not teach any psychology. We meet, however, the same ideas we have been interested in, in the new Subject, Nature-worship, viz., Nature-worthship.

For the time being we will talk about Nature as if she were something essentially different from soul. She is not different. The so-called objective world is to me, and ought to be to you only an EXTENSION of the Human. Look at the landscape—it is not a mass of dead matter, so-called. It is a soul, it moves, it speaks to us, it impresses us with greatness and a longing for the Infinite. It behaves divinely. "The world is an idea of the self-existing." "The earth is all enchanted ground." "The world is a man, and man is a world." "The World, like a radiation, is not and cannot be separated from the sum of the substance of the mighty God."¹ You can say

> I am all this visible earth;
> I am all this visible sky;
> I am all this visible fire;
> I am all this visible wind;
> I am all this visible ocean—
> It is I that *made* all this ocean-girt world;
> It is I that *became* all this ocean-girt world.
> It is I that *own* all this ocean-girt world.²

¹Desatir: ²Omar Khayam: ²Nammahvar Tirnvoymozhi in the "Awakening of India."

*Inorganic nature, as such, does not exist.* It is organized, and is, as it were, the universal germ, the matrix, out of which organization proceeds. The organization of each body is but the internal evolution of the body itself; the earth, by its own evolving, becomes animal and plant. And yet the organic world *has not formed itself* out of the inorganic, but was, at least potentially, present in it from the beginning. What now lies before us apparently as inorganic matter, is the residuum of an organic metamorphosis, is that which at first trial was unable to become organic. All things are internally identical and the potential presence is the same in all. The so-called dead matter is an animal world, a plant world asleep; sometime in the future it may wake up and animate.

Nature is visible mind and mind is invisible nature. In the idea of the absolute ideality of the mind within us and nature without us lies the solution of the problem how it is possible for a nature outside of us to be. Nature is a copy, a *Doppelbild*, of the mind, which the mind itself produces in order to discover itself. The mind sees itself everywhere; sees as H. C. Andersen did so naïvely, the man in the plant and the animal; sees, as the poetic and mystic mind does, "the father's face," the Human, everywhere, sees as A. Oehlenschläger did the Gospel in the stone and running brook, in the mist and in the green leaves. You all know how Coleridge and Wordsworth in particular expressed this view, how they saw the Human or Mind everywhere. *The key to Nature is the psychic factor. The key to the human life is the heart.* Everything is symbolical of the soul. The Ego, the Human, is the true Absolute.

Matter is simply a name for the Abyss, whence flows "the stuff," viz., EXTENSION for Deity, but both "the stuff" and the abyss are one. Matter is thus Human, for Human is the right name for the Universal. We only KNOW the Human.

In psalms Man utters his innermost emotions and finds rest by the utterance, for all utterance is creation and all creation is rest.

In Holy Books Man records his experiences and in their reflection finds Himself, though he sometimes mistakes the vision for another.

In creeds Man formulates his inner life; and in churches Man organizes his forces; in liturgies and rituals he expresses his religious emotions. These creeds, churches and liturgies are often so spontaneous that Man takes them for what he calls revelations from extra-human sources, but time and growth clear his mind and he sees himself and his own mind's products.

All these forms are HUMAN and beyond that HUMAN there is nothing.

It is the same power—the Human or the Divine in manifestation—which as sunbeams call the animal and vegetable world into being and which creates and re-creates the moral law in our hearts.

It is the same power—the Human—which calls the flower to open itself and which turns the inner eye to seek the all-good and all-true.

It is the same power—the universal Human—which covers the ruins with moss, to hide its ugliness, and which throws the mantle of forgiveness over a wasted life.

It is the same power—the Human—which draws the spring from the mountain side and which opens the wells of love in the heart.

All circles of life run into one another, and like Dante's vision they reveal innermost the Human.

> Everywhere a Human Mind and a Human Heart!
> The intelligent forms of ancient poets,
> The fair humanities of old religion.
> The Power, The Beauty, and the Majesty,
> That had their haunts in dale, in piny mountain,
> Or forest by slow stream, or pebbly spring,
> Or chasms or wat'ry depths; all these have vanish'd;
> They live no longer in the faith of reason!
> But still the heart doth need a language, still
> Doth the old instinct bring back the old names,
> And to yon starry world they now are gone,
> Spirits or gods, that used to share this earth
> With man as with their friend; and to the lover
> Yonder they move, from yonder visible sky
> Shoot influence down; and even at this day
> 'Tis Jupiter who brings whate'er is great,
> And Venus who brings everything that's fair!
> —Schiller's Wallenstein; tr. by Coleridge.

Because the Nature man, the free man, feels the Human everywhere, he worth-ships it. It is the highest possible reality which a living being can realize. The Human is to him the character and type of the thing. The Human has not arisen from the thing; the thing has come into existence by way of the Human; is an emanation from the Human. The Human comes first in the descending scale of serial emanation; afterward comes the thing, *and comes in the image of man*. Existence is a system of relations; first comes the self, then the not-self. Man in the plenitude of his being, or, the Human, is his own end.

How natural, then, that he worth-ships nature, and can do naught else. Though arrogant and foolish individuals may deny it, they are still bound up so with nature, that only by placing themselves in a worth-shipful attitude can they come to rest. The Gita says truly: "This world is not for him who does not worship." No one can understand, enjoy or realize their own lives who does not worth-ship; "all the world is love's dwelling." (Hafiz.) The ancient gods of nature are not dead; they have been turned into demons and now they torment the *blasé*. No worn out soul, no one in conflict with himself, can enjoy nature. How could he? He is in contradiction to himself.

> Let me not know the change
> O'er Nature thrown by guilt!—the boding sky,
> The hollow leaf-sounds ominous and strange,
> The weight wherewith the dark tree-shadows lie!

What poor, blind mortals those around us whom city life and business have destroyed, whose dim sight cannot see that all nature is symbolic of man, and have never observed that "the earth changes like a human face."

> " \* \* man, once descried, imprints forever
> His presence on all lifeless things: the winds
> Are henceforth voices, wailing or a shout,
> A querulous mutter or a quick, gay laugh,
> Never a senseless gust  \* \*
> The herded pines commune and have deep thoughts:
> A secret they assemble to discuss
> When the sun drops behind their trunks which glare
> Like gates of hell: the peerless cup afloat
> Of the lake-lily is an urn, some nymph
> Swims bearing high above her head  \* \*
> The morn has enterprise; deep quiet droops
> With evening; triumph takes the sunset hour;
> Voluptuous transport ripens with the corn
> Beneath a warm moon like a happy face:
> And this to fill us with regard for man  \* \* "\*

\*Browning: Paracelsus.

When we come out into the fields or out upon the ocean, in among the mountains, we are under the proper surroundings in which "to pray" for that which we long, that which is to come, because Nature is the Becoming, the Coming. In those places we are in the right environment and can best hear our own voice and heart beat. If our sigh returns as ashes upon our tongue, we have surely asked for the wrong. If the wide vista of transparent air does not open up to show us a vision, our position is false. If the glorious Sun, Zeus in almighty and allwise manifestation, does not smile encouragingly, we may know that our wish is not true and good.

Let me tell you a story. Two lovers walked abroad in the fields to look at the distant hills. The hills so fascinated them that they simultaneously conceived the idea to go up into them. It is always inspiring to go up into a mountain. They wanted to go up a hill, just before them, the highest of them all, as if to an altar, there to offer prayer for liberation from present bondage, and freedom to join hands and hearts openly in the world. Secretly they were one and always have been, but only lately affinity had brought them together. They reached the mountain and they climbed it. Her smile and ecstasy encouraged him and his strong arm lifted her. They told of their longings for each other; how they had searched far and wide in the crowd, in the king's palace, in the farm, in the market-place, and everywhere. How they had looked and now and then thought that they had found. The spirits of rock and tree led them into their secrets and they dreamt of far gone periods of existence. She told him how she recognized in him a remembrance of a past hero and he said that she appeared to him a realization of that ideal woman, who always came to him in dreams. When they came to a promontory and the open country lay before them with its villages, rivers and forests, they vowed to travel together through the world to see all that beauty. At last they reached the top and before them lay the vision of the distant horizon, enclosing their present prison of uncongenial companions, but also a promise that their future was as wide and enclosed as many possibilities of happiness as the surrounding country enclosed various objects. They were weary from the struggle in bondage and weary of the climb, but they were happy.

A refreshing rest, a love embrace, a sigh and the descent began. The sun was calling the evening hour of prayer. They stopped on a rocky promontory and looked into the sun asking the sphinx for a word to remember. Just then the sun shone more gloriously than at any time of the day. Warmth and love came riding on mountain mist and the panorama revealed forms of bliss. They saw themselves as ethereal spirits ascending and they bowed down before Nature's throne and felt a blessing being given. He spoke first and said: "Here before thee, glorious orb, my elder brother, I declare this woman to be my wife, for I have found her and she is my own soul. Thou art above; here below and upon this rock on which we stand, I say that I have known her always and that we are more firmly bound than the particles of this rock, we stand upon. In the presence of these trees, which are the ladder to heaven, called out of the rocks by Thee, Great Sun, I swear fidelity and claim my rights." And she said: "Amen—yes, so it is, so it was, and so it shall be. I kiss this leaf and throw it into the valley below. It is my message, I send into the Abyss. It binds me! It is my testimony. Glorious Sun, I thank Thee! Now I can bear my chains; they are no more chains. I am happy." While they spoke they stood arm in arm and when they kissed each other, the birds sang their best song. The evening was solemn and the night divine. They remember the mountain and their declarations: *their* mountain, *their* declaration. *Within a few months they married.*

A member: Are we not under the influence of the stars?

Lecturer: You ask me about nativities, influences of the stars, and what not. Your questions seem to imply that you take for granted that you are RULED by natural circumstances and not free to carve your own fortune.

I protest against such an explanation of our existence. We are free spirits and not naturalistic elements. An Ingersoll may talk about Jehovah's brutalities, but his picturesque delineations are nothing compared to the pictures we should have to paint if Necessity really ruled us as the astrologers would have us believe. There is something radically wrong in Astrology as popularly taught. We are only to a limited extent dependent upon and resting upon the "order of things." Life is certainly a current that carries us along with it, but we can also cross the stream, yea, we can sail against both current and wind. It is true that the fox grows gray, but never good, and that the crab-tree does not bear pippins. But above those laws rules the Self, and the Self is essentially free. Freedom is its very essence. In Self is both form, will and contents. Out of itself, by itself, for itself, it constructs its own world. The laws of nature do not rule the Self; Self is freedom, will, poise, character, beauty. It is man's world and *man is master*. He is born to be master. Sovereignty is his birthright.

I protest against the modern revival of Karma. We do not want to see the old stage paraphernalia again. We live in a new world, a world of loving service, truthfulness, purity, obedience and love, and all these virtues spring from man himself. We do not draw from Necessity. Our world is full of goodness; the very air we breathe is surcharged with wisdom and love. We draw from the infinite stores, the infinite reservoirs, the ideals, and we sail upon the ocean of mercy. Our pilot never sleeps and his mighty arm never grows weary.

I grant that two worlds are ours, but the ideal world, I maintain, is the real and the strongest. We will not, we cannot, any longer drift as logs with the varying tides of natural life. We hoist our sail, we get up steam and we sail according to the dictates of our true humanity.

It is true, that most of us have to fight to maintain that freedom. It is true that from an everyday standpoint we seem to lie in mid-air, and our position seems unsafe. But how can that really be? What is firmer and safer than the Deity? We are in the Deity when we are free.

When I talk about Nature worship—nature-worthship—there is always a perplexing problem that comes up before my mind. Is she not sometimes wanton? Is she perhaps fiendish? Certainly she does seem reckless in the way she destroys her own work. Let me quote from my daybook:

"In 1870 I spent my vacation, together with a number of fellow students, on the heaths of Jutland. We came out with the purpose of camping on the heath. Before we could perfect our arrangements, we spent a few days with a miller near the romantic and historic lake of Hall, near Viborg. From this place we took daily rambles in various directions among the hills, in order, so to say, to get used to the monotony of a heath landscape.

One hot July afternoon we started out to walk about ten miles due south into the heath, to return late by the moonlight, so to see what a night on the heath looked like. But the fates were against us, for we had scarcely walked four miles, when by turning round we were startled by seeing in the distance heavy volumes of smoke rise from the ground. As far as we could locate the probable fire, it was in the direction of the plantings on the hills southwest of Hall Lake. With one voice we uttered a despairing cry, for intuitively we felt the impending danger.

Though intensely sorry for the destructions that would follow the consuming march of the flames, we could not but admire the wonderful effect of the sunlight upon the smoke. It rose heavy and dark, only relieved here and there by some white circling lines, but as these circles ascended, they reflected the sun in exquisite green tints, sometimes changing to yellow, sometimes becoming more reddish, when the wind fanned the flames higher up. The smoke seemed to keep hanging in the air, like clouds, and little by little they covered the whole horizon. Evidently the fire was of large dimensions and covered an extensive area of land. For hours we stood silently watching the spectacle, before we started toward the fire. It seemed to be Nature's best efforts in color blending, and for us new studies in chromatic effects. She seemed to be planning new combinations of tints not known to man, and as she could indulge her ease in regard to time, for no man could put down the fire, she first tried the effects of the midday sun, but found time, too, to study her fiery transformations of the landscape in sunset and pale moonlight, and sunrise as well. With grim satisfaction she seemed to enjoy her work, for the sunset was magnificent, and the moonlight of the night was as calm and elevating as any. Peace and quiet rested everywhere, except on the burning hills, where the trees lost their lives as if they were cast into a burning and seething oven, and where the despairing cries of the small creeping things of the earth were unheard in the roar of the flames.

It was at least four miles away and we should not reach it before night. We started at last, and set out with a will to help, if our help could do anything to arrest such a fire, that seemed to be surging as a flood over acres upon acres. Upon arrival we found our anticipations verified. The old plantations of pine and spruce were burning and nothing could be done to stop the flames, because the ground was burning, too. The peat and dry vegetable matter in which the trees grew had now become an unconquerable enemy to the trees. The only prospect of an end to the fire lay in the fire reaching the foot of the hills, where it would extinguish itself in the lake. Roaring in its intense fury, the fire wreathed itself in glittering rings round the pine trunks, and, bursting with loud thunder, it fell as one broad blaze upon the foliage of the yet untouched trees. Though no wind nourished the flames, they fanned themselves into fury, and rolling along the inflammable soil, it consumed everything before it over a tract of land a thousand yards long and a little less wide, leaving only a few charred trunks and roots and the raw, blackened soil behind it. It burned all night, and not till evening the next day was it satiated, and that only because it reached the lake. The last burning trees fell in the water as if the fire had run itself mad and would attempt the existence of another element.

What is the philosophy of this, was asked, and an expression of opinion was freely given. Almost all voted that this fire was a fiendish act of nature and a national calamity.

The soil on these heaths is in many places only a foot or two deep. Below it is Ahl or sand. The horn of an angry bull will rip it open and let out the dreaded sand, and the hoof of a horse will force it out.

A national calamity! How much time, labor and cost had not the government spent upon this tract of land to raise some vegetation on it! The soil is too "chalky" for grass, otherwise these heaths would have become prairies long ago. Now they will only grow the heather, and the common broom, and, where, after long seasons of patient toil, some foundation for diminutive trees have been made, the government plants them. It had taken centuries to prepare the soil for these firs and spruce, and they themselves had struggled hard enough for a hold upon existence. Now in a few hours all this had been destroyed and lost. It will take other centuries to make a soil out of decomposed heather, deep and rich enough to nourish the poor shrubs that fight for light in it.

Our excursion had been spoiled, so from the now black and desolate hills we returned to the mill to resume our journey the next morning. In the evening we very naturally discussed the calamity of the fire and general sadness prevailed. A sadness very much to the credit of the company, for it showed its patriotism and demonstrated very clearly that all comprehended the nature of the loss. Nobody can realize this who does not know what scarcity of timber means on the heath, or who has never seen the shifting sands break loose from under the soil and destroy his gardens and plantings.

I myself did not take much part in the discussion, but delivered myself in the course of the evening of the following little speech. "It is easy enough," I said, "to point to nature's cruelty and show the martyrdom of all creation. It is not difficult to discover decline and death all around us. The heath itself is an example upon the penury of nature, if you so will. But this is only one side of nature. Wherever there is decrease, there is also increase; life and death follow upon one another in a ceaseless round. Nature swings between two extremes and repeats herself. It may also be charged that she never directly produces the Immortal. It is true she often destroys in a few hours all the works of her hands for many years. We have just seen such a case. With absolute indifference to consequences she submerges large tracts of land by earthquakes or by floods and recklessly she kills scores by pestilence. These facts are only too well known. All this is true, but I maintain that she cannot act otherwise. It is so her law. All her doings are "one against another." It has been beautifully said, that nature is a "system of nuptials," always endeavoring to multiply life. One might as truthfully say that she is death, always endeavoring to destroy the very life, she has produced. Every man's experience has proved that to his own satisfaction, and the Orientals have expressed this great truth in their mythology. Siva, the symbol of the destructive powers of life, is an equal of Brahma, the creative power. I repeat, therefore, and say that nature can do no otherwise. She is blind and acts unconsciously. And from this standpoint I excuse and defend her.

I have admitted that nature never directly produces the Immortal, and from that standpoint I am willing to criticise, but not from any other. And even here I will act and speak with caution. If she cannot teach us directly, she can do it by means of riddles, indirectly, or in dark hieroglyphics write man a text about immortal life, though she can neither interpret him the text, nor give him a key to it. Let me explain this by a few examples from the life of the plants. Some gentle hand, for instance, breaks off a lily in the garden. An act, by the way, equal to murdering a human being, for it is taking from that plant the aim and object of all its vital energies, an object as valuable to the plant as life is to man. The lily, however, is not yet discouraged; in honest toil it renews its efforts, and soon sends forth new flowers, one after another, from the small side branchlets. This the plant does always if its structure permits and its vitality has not been exhausted in the first effort. Certainly it would never have done it but for the destruction of the first born. Thus the lily testifies to its belief in its power to survive destruction. It teaches quietly the lesson that it will and cannot cease to labor till it shall have done its work. And what is this but Nature's belief in immortality? To be sure it is not the crude idea of being called out of the grave with a body like the one laid down into it. It is a much nobler and far-reaching thought. It reveals a state of mind which rests in the idea, that time is only a phenomenal appearance and that the soul which lives to-day shall also live to-morrow. But to expect to live to-morrow is psychologically the same as to expect to live always. The emphasis is upon your *expectation*, not upon the form you may assume to-morrow.

Again, go into the fields; you see it right here on the heath, and you observe that wherever the cattle have bitten off the young green flower-heads new shoots are coming forth from every joint below. They crop out by the dozen to substitute the single one broken off. Is that not wonderful? But these illustrations are not single instances, parallels may be found throughout Nature's various kingdoms, and they all show how far she is able to hint at spiritual truth and to foreshadow it."

Here my speech was suddenly broken off. It seemed to the audience that I was about to defend and exalt Nature, to which they objected unanimously.

We must be merged in the Beloved to know the Beloved. We must love Nature to understand Nature's love.

When I was young I was fond of the heath, and quite at home among the heathers, and enjoyed the noiseless desert. I felt the power of loneliness and was under its spell. The loneliness put me in relation to the penetration of Nature and by way of the "little things" I learned to worship Nature. Here is an extract from my daybook:

"As I lie here among the heathers, I wonder at the origin of the delicate color of their little flowers. All so noble, and made with equal care and allotted an equal share of brightness. How and when did they get it and where and when did this all-comprehending loving kindness, which did it, acquire its skill? I do not only wonder, but I admire, and my admiration grows to reverent love. As I grow ecstatic, Nature becomes more personal and eloquent. There is a sermon of love and praise in these little flowers. The difference between this sermon of Nature's and that of the minister is, that he is merely a professor and talks too much, while Nature's preaching is really a conversation and her subject is always that of her listener's heart. Her words suit always the occasion and you feel she knows what she talks about, though she cannot express all she knows. Her eloquence is so quiet and simple, that you instinctively confide in her.

This heath is not lonesome to me. I am by my Beloved. I am alone with Nature. We are alone by ourselves, and as two lovers we may enjoy those little details of life, which are so interesting to lovers, because they are so personal and so private. They are little things, but after all they are closely connected with the great events of our life. The more we can learn to keep ourselves face to face with the simple and pretty little things of Nature, the nearer we shall come to her heart. Truly they are wonderful, and I was never surprised at the exclamation of the Sufi poet: Cleave an atom, and in it, you shall find a world. Indeed the infinitely small is as marvelous as the infinitely great. The mystery of the starry heavens is no greater than the mystery of the making of a heather flower here upon the sandy desert of Jutland.

Like all lovers, Nature is quite jealous of these little common things. They show her privacy and she wants them recognized. But ah! men are too dull. It takes a cataclysm of worlds to wake him up, and then he forgets it next day, anyhow.

I fancy all lovers trace out the *beginnings* of their love; it would be so natural if they did. It would certainly be a delightful pastime, I imagine. I ask Nature about the beginning of her love and she answers me, that she saw me, when I was made in secret, and curiously wrought in the lowest parts of the earth. I endeavor to imagine this wonderful love, but give up, not in despair, but in perfect confidence to the truth of her word. The truth is, we never see beginnings. Who can trace, for instance, a river to its start—its *first* start? Nobody can do it. It really does not begin in the spring, which we point to. The spring is only a concentration of the innumerable little drops that fall from the moss and from the trees and trickle down the hillside to the spring. And where did these drops come from, but from the clouds? And the clouds, did they come all from the ocean? Did not some of them, or perhaps the largest part of their substance, exist from *the* Beginning? But what was back of *that* beginning, I know not. Push my query back as far as I may, I find not the beginning of Nature's love. She loved always; she is love."

I have grown enthusiastic, but a lover's enthusiasm is excusable.

This is the Lord's own day.
I stand alone in the wide field.
It is as if a multitude
Knelt down and prayed with me.



—Move along these shades
In gentleness of heart; with gentle hand
Touch—for there is a spirit in the woods.



—These trees shall be my books.—

# SEVENTH LECTURE.

Let us sink back into ourselves for a few moments. Close your eyes and sit perfectly still.

### INVOCATION.

"May that soul of mine and that of yours, which is a ray of the divine light of the great universal love, be united by devout meditations with that Infinite Light whence we have come. May we for a moment or two sink back into the Great All and stand in Being. May we now and hereafter live that universal life which is to live the true life, and may the Great All light upon us, and may the Great All, in its manifestations shine upon us, and may the Great All, combining the spirit of the first and the second powers, lead us through this existence."

The subject is again Nature worship. We ought, of course, to have been outdoors and under the pines. But the weather will not allow us. You must make the best of it and think yourself out there among the trees. Forget that you are in the city and that it is winter.

I will give you a symbol, which antiquity and the modern world can agree in calling the unit of existence. The symbol is the pine cone.

But before I explain the wonders of the cone, let me speak of the pine tree. I will not merely tell you some scientific facts, I will speak of the pine because of its human traits. "We are plants," said Plato, and it is true in more than a figurative sense. We are plants, and it is therefore that no place is so eloquent as a forest.

> There is a power, a presence in the woods;
> A viewless Being, that with life and love
> Informs the reverential solitudes;
> The rich air knows it, and the mossy sod—

The pine grove especially is sacred ground. The very light that streams through the dim and dewy veil of the foliage has a cathedral air about it, and the tremulous sounds that come from the pine needles whisper awful secrets. It behooves us to wander with reverence, for we are among witnesses as old as the earliest vegetable growth on earth, and the pine is the most universal of all trees. It represents in all zones and forms as Oken has said so significantly, "the mountain's roof."

Botanically, the pine is a most peculiar and interesting tree, and it is as such that it can be so helpful to us in leading us back toward the origin of things. Its primitivity is seen in its simplicity of fructification, which is similar to the lowly club-moss, that creeps along among the heathers. That which is transitory in the higher trees is here permanent. The pine stands in its arrested growth as a bridge from far remote ages, and over it we may travel back and see many mysteries on the other side. One mystery is that peculiar darkness that broods over the pine wood. We must study it! Another is those dirge-like tones we hear in those woods. We must study them! In those mournful murmuring sounds, now low, now soft, ever varying with the rising and falling breeze, we ought to be led into that holiness of melancholy so characteristic for the prophet. The sough of the wind fanning the air over the many edges suggests ruins, and we seem transferred to the ages of cataclysms and great upheavals. So consistent with its symbology is the pine, that is has no leaves, but only stalks for leaves. Its cone is the arrested flowerbud of higher trees. The Bible speaks of the Cedars of the Lord both as a phallic emblem, and with reference to the pine as the oldest of all trees on the earth. When the gods walked the earth, I imagine they walked in sacred groves of pines. The *lycopod* at our foot is a contemporary of the pine, and both made the carboniferous period. As if all these facts were not enough evidence that we are on sacred ground, the pine clothes itself in evergreen robes. Time seems to have no existence with it.

The pine has two names, which also associate it with the Remote. The Latin *pinus* comes, it is thought, from the Celtic *ben, pin*, even to this day preserved in Ben-Lomond, etc. It means the mountain. Its name *fir* is derived from fir, fyr, fire, still found in *fire*wood. Indeed, a fir is fire in more than one respect. Of that later.

The pine is the ideal pattern of a tree; it is like a flame in shape, hence holy among Assyrians, etc. Its conical shape is admirably adapted for securing stability, etc.

Now, about the pine cone. Let me mix my own observations with notes taken freely from Hugh MacMillan, Flammarion and other authors.

There is one thing you want to fix in your mind, because it lies at the root of all movement, and that is the spiral. The earth describes a spiral, and has never yet passed twice through the same point of space. With the solar system of ours, the earth moves spirally, and in an oblique direction toward the constellation Hercules. To you sensitives, do not these words "spiral" and "oblique" direction convey worlds of meaning? Do they not fascinate you? Do you not feel the mighty gyrational movements of the universe? Do you not perceive—almost literally perceive—the law of force that determines the form of all organic bodies? The animal and vegetable kingdoms are built on that law; it appears in the cell, it can be traced in all the leaves in the calyx, coralla, stamen and seed vessels. The leaves are wound around the stem of a plant in a spiral; our own heart is a form of the spiral principle. The spiral is the form of rest; it gives greatest security, a maximum of contents with a minimum of exposure.

Human history moves in cycles, viz., at every turn of the upward or forward movement of the world-spiral we come to repetitions, but add a new element. Let me show these cycles in history and individuals. You will learn quietness from them. It is so often difficult for us to realize that a forward movement is safe. We grow uneasy at the whirl of life, and fear the new in its destructive force, because we do not know the law of progress. Progress is spiral, and we ought to come to rest with the knowledge that such is the law of force, and it is that law of force which works both good and evil; evil to him who doubts and fears, good to him who is free and courageous. The double truth veiled in the spiral movement—of which the pine cone is such a marvelous emblem—the ancients expressed by the famous phrase, "vortex rules." The fearful said—when the stability of things seemed gone, that Zeus had gone on a trip to Ethiopia and that vortex ruled, which to them meant, that all was swept away in the whirlpool of moving forces. Do not be afraid! Your ship cannot go down! No soul ever drowned! Much "impurity" comes up from the abyss and seemingly pollutes the clear waters. In our own day, the slimy weeds of "nastiness" come up, strangely mixed with new and beautiful forms. Many barren and lifeless fragments float upon the tides, giving evidence of miscarriages in some psychic sphere.

However this may be, the interest centers in the activity of the Vortex, and it becomes a question of importance, if we *can discern a rational, systematic and scientific basis for the currents.* A basis, satisfactory alike to the scholar, the artist, the literary man, and the religious? Is the Vortex instinct with fresh life or does it mean death?

I believe there is a sound and healthy life behind—even the erotic literature of to-day; and I know, it can be shown, satisfactorily, what causes the declination of the erotic currents.

In like manner I know there is truth as well as falsity behind the modern mind-cure methods, and theosophic vagaries; the socialistic and industrial upheavals, etc. These forms look like lawlessness, but are not entirely so. I believe that vortex whirls both good and bad into our actual existence.

When Aristophanes makes Socrates say that Zeus is no more and that Vortex rules, he utters neither a sarcasm nor a witticism, but, borrowing the philosophy from Anaxagoras, he gives a *symbolical* description of a law of existence. Zeus' absence means that apparent withdrawal of the *principle of balance*, which we observe historically at the end of every age or historical period. And the rule of vortex means the bubbling up of the new elements of the coming civilization.

This I will try to show by examples. I will begin by describing the Vortex, so admirably defined by Jacob Boehme.

It is well known to all of you that the Old Testament speaks about God in anthrophomorphic and physical terms, which are shocking to those who think in more *spiritual* conceptions or mental forms. I think, however, a true theosophic study of the subjects will admit all three sides as necessary in the Deity.

For my present purpose I shall dwell upon the physical definitions given in the Old Testament.

God is *fire* and *light*, in a sense the most actual of all. He is a *consuming fire* and his *wrath* has *flaming fire* as its result. Scripture does not hesitate to name God not only the former of light, but also as creator of *darkness* (Is. 45. 7) and where it describes the manifestation of the divine glory, it distinguishes in it *darkness, fire, and light*.

It seems to me most interesting to observe this naturalism in the Bible, for it corresponds so perfectly to the notions of the old philosophers, the mystics and the mediæval theosophists, all of which have been accused of an uncritical mixing up of God and the world in their pantheistic philosophy.

Boehme starts from an observation common enough to us all. We find everywhere two qualities, one good and one evil, which in this world exist together in all powers and all creatures. In the opposition of the two qualities arises a rotatory motion, or vortex, productive of all the forms of life which we know. This vortex is a fountain, whence flows actual existence. His description is too long to give here in details, but his imagery is grand. The two opposite forces he describes as fountain spirits inflaming themselves, frantically foaming and tearing one another, when from amidst of them arises, through the violent conflict, the region of this world, partaking of the natures of both, wrath, fire and darkness. His imagery suggests the grand natural epic of Norse Mythology which sings about the fiery and violent Muspelheim and the nebular and dark Nifelheim, with the Ginungagap between them, out of which arises the actual world.

Boehme's vortex is always in motion, it is eternally rising, bubbling up, and bringing forth. Creation has never ceased. The fire wheel is ever turning and casting up rudiments of new forms, and ideas to new creations. From this vortex comes all the new life of to-day.

May be, some of us, "see no divinity in grass, no life in dead stone, nor spirit in the air," but no matter, the unknown tongues are understood by the initiated, and even modern science has got a glimpse of the vortex. Its nebular theory assumes fiery gyrations and turbulent activity as preceding the present state of matter.

Boehme has a predecessor in his philosophy, the old Greek, Anaxagoras, though he did not know it.

*Anaxagoras* declared that genesis and decay in the strict sense are unthinkable, that genesis consists merely in the combination, and all decay in the separation, of substances already in existence. The motion with which a combination and separation takes place is rotatory. The whirling motion is never ending and is the central moving factor throughout creation.

Of course, this dry description does not call up before the mind's eye any very living picture, but it means very much to him who can throw himself into it, and by means of his image-making powers can perceive the pulse of the universe.

If I may be allowed a sudden descent from Universals to Particulars, I would say that the pulsation might be compared to the phenomena of volcanic eruptions: the expansive force of great masses of imprisoned and uprushing volumes of vapors forcing a passage for themselves through solid rock-masses, *lead to shocks, jars and displacements,* which again give rise to what is known as earthquakes, and finally terminate in flaming eruptions.

These shocks, jars, and displacements, usually follow one another in regular succession, almost like the throbbing of the pulse. If we throw off childish fear at such an occasion and approach nature in confidence, we shall readily feel the beating heart of that fire world which lies at our feet, and be initiated in the mysteries of vortex.

If we will understand and feel that *Presence*

> "Whose dwelling is the light of setting suns,
> And the round ocean, and the living air,
> And the blue sky, and in the mind of Man,"

we must arouse our dull senses and come away from the conventional schools and descend with Faust to *the Mothers*, the fountain spirits; then shall we be "immersed in the ocean of vision" and behold "the form of His beauty."

Such is the teaching of the Mystic, to whom Nature is instinct with divine life. He recognizes the impress of the divine face upon every atom. *Nature to him is a process by which the Absolute realizes itself, unfolds itself, and—infolds itself: vortex.*

There is another congenial spirit, I like to mention: Heraclit. He too is one who attained the vision and yet lived to tell the tale.

He does not so much describe the vortex itself as the stream that flows from vortex, that never ending fullness, which casts up upon the shores of life the strangest splendors together with crippled and unhealthy children. He sees the eternal flow, the flux, and uninterrupted movement and transformation; a stream always spreading and yet again collecting itself.

Anaxagoras looks upon Vortex as an eternal chant. Boehme descends to its bottom and describes its turnings, while Heraclit follows the magic tread from the abyss into this world. In all three we may follow "from link to link," "the soul of all the worlds," the Mother power, vortex.

I have now given you some philosophy on spirals. I shall next show the historical cycles.

This theory of cycles, of which I now speak, is nothing new, it was taught by various Greek philosophers and by the theosophists of the Middle Ages.

Historical cycles require either 250, 500, 700 or 1,000 years to rotate. That is, at the end of so many years we find that events occur, which answer perfectly to the state that exists when "Zeus is no more and Vortex rules." Great catastrophes terminate the past and violent upheavals begin the new age. Darkness, Death and Despair settle low upon the land and the nations tremble. Then comes forth after the Ragnarockur, a new world, amidst great pain and anxiety and mostly always in bloodshed.

I will describe an "historical wave" or a cycle of 250 years' duration.

We begin in China 2,000 B. C., in the "golden age" of the empire, the age of philosophy and reforms.

Two hundred and fifty years later, or 1750 B. C., the Mongolians establish a powerful empire in Central Asia.

Two hundred and fifty years later, or 1500 B. C., Egypt rises from its temporary degradation and extends its sway over many parts of Europe and Asia.

Twelve hundred and fifty B. C., or 250 years afterward, the wave reaches and crosses over to Eastern Europe, filling it with the spirit of the Argonautic Expeditions, and dies out in 1000 B. C. at the siege of Troy.

Look up these dates in history and you will find, as I said, that night settled for a time upon the earth and that a new day broke forth only through violent commotions.

About 1000 B. C. vortex turns up a second historical wave in Central Asia and culminates toward the year 750 B. C., when the Scythians leave their steppes and sweep down upon the adjoining countries, destroying the old and breaking forcibly an opening for the new world life. Two hundred and fifty years later, or about 500 B. C., an epoch of splendor begins in Ancient Persia. From thence the wave moves on still further West and in 250 B. C. reaches Greece in her highest state of culture and civilization, the mistress of the world of Beauty and Spirit. Two hundred and fifty years later bring us to the birth of the Christ and the apogee of the Roman empire. The historical student will find less difficulty in verifying these data than those of the former historical wave. He will easily see that at the given dates the respective nations and kingdoms play the representative parts. He will also easily recognize the terrible "woes" and "cups of wraths" which the new births cost to bring forth.

At about the beginning of our era, vortex is again active and a third historical wave sweeps on from the far East. After many revolutions, about this time, China forms once more a powerful empire, both politically, commercially, socially and in the world of arts and sciences. Two hundred and fifty years later, the wheel of existence forces the Huns upon the scene—and their name is devastation and crude might; while it raises up a new and powerful Persian Kingdom in 500 A. D.; a Byzantine empire in 750; and a second Roman tyranny, the Papacy, in the year 1000; in which year it reaches a most extraordinary degree of power and wealth.

At the same time vortex starts a *fourth* stream from the ever rotating whirlpool called vortex, approaches from the Orient, where China is once more flourishing. Two hundred and fifty years later, or 1250 A. D., the Mongolian wave from Central Asia has overflowed and devastated enormous tracts of land, Russia included. With fatal necessity, we find the ever turning wheel, in 1500 raise the Ottoman empire in might and abandons the Balkan peninsula to its sway. About this time Russia frees itself from the Tartar and in 1750 rises to unexpected height and glory under Catharina II; and who knows but that Napoleon's prophecy may come true that at the end of the fixed 250 years or at the year 2000 the Muscovite may rule Europe? At any rate, in that year 2000 we may expect great historical changes—and no doubt we see now the beginning of the end. Seventeen hundred and eighty-nine and the French revolution are no doubt the key to the present situations and they contain the germs for the coming cataclysms and the incoming of the "Millennium."

Here, then, you have a continuous series of cycles. To see fully the new elements that come into history you need only to write these cycles upon an enlarged copy of the historical diagram given you in the Spring lectures.

All this wonderful spiral philosophy you can see in a pine cone. The pine cone shows it all. You can therefore not wonder that the ancient nature worshipers revered the cone and that it was an emblem of life in so many mythologies.

The spiral is the circle infinitely continued. The circle returns upon itself, ending where it began, but the spiral has neither beginning nor end. It is a cosmological law. It is an emblem of eternity. You, who use the circle as such an emblem, are quite in error.

The great lesson the cone illustrates is the simplicity of nature, the multitude and boundless variety of results, which she educes from one self-evident law, a law affecting the stars, the heart of man, history, etc.

Cut a cone horizontally, you get a circle; cut it diagonally, you get an ellipse or hyperbola. Divide a cone through the middle, from top to bottom, and the inner surface of each half is a triangle. In that half which arises from the cutting a cone from top to bottom you get the shape and the formation of a flame. Light a candle and place it alongside of such a cone and you see in each the four divisions of fire-life. Symbolically the flame and the cone are synonymous. If you see in the cone the fire-life of the soul, you can also understand why I am so enthusiastic about a cone.

It is to be believed that all the orbs of heaven have similar numerical relations to each other as the spiral arrangement of the parts of plants, and that the whole universe is arranged on the same principle which we observe in the pine cone.

> Yes, all things
> Are numbered in a calculation far
> Beyond the reach of Newton, or Laplace.

"God geometrizes incessantly." "The life of God is mathematical."

I beg you to go into the woods "to think the thoughts of God." By means of a pine-cone you can ascend to the Deity. The pine wood is the most lively cathedral for Nature worship. In Nature the mind of God meets the mind of man. In the woods, by holding a cone in your hand, your *own number* will be revealed. In the woods you stand on holy ground.

"Thou hast ordered all things in measure, and number, and weight."—Wisdom, XI, 20.

*Love is the cause and aim of all things.*

> *O dear God above
> This beautiful but sad perplexing earth,
> Pity the hearts that know—or know not love!*
>          *E. W. Wilcox.*

*Plato says that Love is the interpreter and mediator between things human and things divine.*

# EIGHTH LECTURE.

Isidor Orient said truly: "Love is the ladder on which we climb to godliness." But what did he mean by love? Love can be both life and death, both crown and curse, both physical, intellectual and spiritual.

Love is the source whence flows all knowledge of God, Freedom and Immortality.

Read Thomas á Kempis on love. Read Algernon Sidney on love. But, better than reading, is to love Love, for many lessons on Love can only be learned that way. Love is not simply vibration, not simply the ripple marks of waves on the shore—wiped out by the next wave. There is something physical about all love, but love is not physical. The essence of love is purity. Love is certainly the great instrument of nature, but it is informed by God. Love is the *deus ex machina* of all things, even the gods are subject to love.

With these words by way of definition, let me read you a paper on Love.

If it be true, as Emerson said, that "all mankind loves a lover," I presume that it will be true that all mankind likes to hear talk about Love.

Mention the word Love, and, strange it is, but something, I know not what, touches a responsive chord in every generous heart. Yes, I may say with the poet,

"All thoughts, all passions, all delights,
Whatever stirs this mortal frame,
All are but ministers of love
And feed his sacred flame."

Certain it is that when once *the heart has opened itself to love*, love returns the favor without stint of measure, for *love then opens the world* to the heart. Indeed, love is a magian and knows the secret of the transmutation of the metal hearts of men. Where love rules, the old things pass away and all things become new. How different do the hills, the valleys, the forests and the ocean look to a lover and to one without rest and peace. Love invests nature with a new glory, throws an enchantment over everything. The all absorbing passion colors every vision, suspends the rules of logic and stimulates intellect to new discoveries. Love once turned a blacksmith to a painter.

To complete the picture! There is one other side! I have a remark to make against that of Emerson's that "all mankind loves a lover." Lovers are selfish. Lord Beaconsfield said truly: "To a man who is in love, the thought of another woman is uninteresting, if not repulsive." That's a selfish sentiment. To lovers, society must give way. They have no eyes nor ears for anybody but themselves. Every book they read and recommend one another has a new charm—to them. But what about everybody else? The words they speak acquire a new meaning—to them. But what about the dictionary? No doubt her song surpasses all other music—to him. But does it electrify anybody else? I will not question that her presence inspires—him. But is her presence a deep moral education? A true woman, whether developed or not, is attracted to a powerful man; that is correct and as it ought to be according to all laws of the universe; but does that attraction enlarge her character, does it give her courage and confidence to trust her passion? If it does, very well; it will deepen and strengthen all her womanly qualities; but if it does not, she becomes a disgrace to herself and a scandal to society.

Well, then, let this be enough for the dark side.

Years ago Hortense Schneider, the "Grand Duchess of Geroldstein," took the part of Boulotte in "Barbe-Bleu," and used to eat real cherries, even though they were out of season and had to be brought from afar at great expense. Every evening she would toss a cherry-stone to the audience, and he who secured it would preserve it as a precious souvenir. It was the fashion with the men to mount such stones in rings, etc. A certain gentleman, who was so happy as to catch one of the stones, instead of mounting it in a ring, planted it in his garden. In a few years he had a vigorous tree and soon choice fruits, a basket of which was thenceforth sent to the *prima donna* every year by her admirer.

A genuine passion may be treated as a precious jewel and mounted on the conventional ring, thus becoming an ornament of life without vitalizing it. It may also be planted deep in the recesses of the heart and become nourishment for the soul.

Only once in a lifetime do we become possessed by an absorbing passion. When it comes, let it be accepted! If we trust a pure passion, we shall find that it deepens and strengthens all human qualities. A great love develops the womanly in woman and the manly in man. When it rises above sensuous passion it touches immortality and lifts its bearers into the ideal realms of Mind, Heart and Nature at large.

I said only once in a lifetime do we become possessed by an absorbing passion. When it comes, let it be accepted. If we turn it away we do it at the peril of our lives.

A great love triumphs over death. The author of "Canticle" tells us that "love is stronger than death."

In the beautiful drama "Ion" (by Talfourd), when the noble Greek is about to surrender his life to the demands of inexorable fate, his beloved Clementhe asks if they shall meet again. The response is: "I have asked that dreadful question of the hills that look eternal—of the clear streams that flow forever—of the stars among whose fields of azure my raised spirit walked in glory. All are dumb. But as I gaze upon thy living face, I feel that there is something in love that rises above its beauty and cannot wholly perish. We shall meet again, Clementhe." A great love triumphs over death.

*Love is said to be strong as death.* Molinos explains this by saying that the love spoken of is *divine* love, and, mystic as he was, he goes into ecstasy at the mere mention of divine love. "The fire of divine love burns the soul," he says; intoxicates it and fills it with unsatisfiableness. Love is said to be strong as death because it kills as death does—*everything earthly.*

But—I am talking about Love, assuming that we all know what Love is. Perhaps I am wrong in that.

I know of no definition I would like to give. Love is too manifold and deep to be inclosed in the casket of a definition. I will therefore avoid definitions and make a few distinctions.

We are all familiar with the classical gods Aphrodite-Venus and Eros, Amor, or Cupid. Which are their dominions and how are they related?

Eros is the universal love—celestial love—the bond of attraction, or, as the modern world would say, the law of attraction that binds the worlds together. He is one of the oldest of gods, coeval with Night, the Abyss.

He is no son of Aphrodite-Venus, nor is he merely Cupid. It was the later poets who made him son of Aphrodite-Venus and drew universal love down to become a mere intrigue and a naughty boy going about shooting arrows at innocent girls' hearts. This idea and office is Eros unworthy.

It is Eros that in the main I speak about in this paper. Yet Eros, universal love, is not out of connection with Love, as we commonly speak of it.

When we say that love is blind we mean, or ought to mean, passionate love, Venus; for the ancients attributed reason and wisdom to Eros.

The ancients that lived before the Greeks and Romans worshipped Eros with great solemnity. They did not think lightly of him nor did they use him for a play toy. To them he was ruler both of the dead and the living and had no parents.

The later art knew of two Cupids, two Eros: Eros, Love,

and Anteros, Love requited. The two Cupids with the dolphin at the foot of the statue of Venus of Medici are supposed to be Eros and Anteros.

Porphyry, the Neoplatonist, tells a pretty legend. Aphrodite complained to Themis that her son (N. B. a false conception) continued always a child. She was told that the reason was his solitariness. If he had a brother companion he would grow. Anteros was soon afterward born, and Eros found his wings enlarge and his person and strength increase. But this was only when Anteros was near; for if he was at a distance, Eros found himself to shrink to his original dimensions.

This legend is as profound as most legends. Experience all over the world proves it true. Only love requited can grow and develop. Love in solitude is death. Love unrequited withers and goes down in suffering. Love unrequited is unhappiness indeed, for it has lost all possibilities for existence.

Though we know of two Eros only, from art representations of a late age and from Porphyry's story, the conception is very old; it is, in fact, coeval with creation. The two loves condition one another.

Love in all its forms hails from Eros or IS Eros. Love, *thus* understood, is indeed the Master Passion, and nothing too exalted can be said about it.

It is Eros that Emilia Viviani speaks about in that magnificent apotheosis, which was the inspiration to Shelley's Epipsychidion. For your benefit I give it here from the edition of Forman, according to Medwin's account.*

*See Forman's ed. of Shelley's poetical works, vol. 2, pages 424-428.

# THE TRUE LOVE.

"Love! soul of the world! Love, the source of all that is good, of all that is lovely! What would the universe be, failing thy creative flame? A horrible desert. But far from this, it is the sole shadow of all goodness, of all loveliness, and of all felicity. Of that love I speak, that possessing itself of all our soul, of our entire will, sublimes and raises one, above every other individual of the same species; and all energetic, all pure, all divine, inspires none but actions that are magnanimous, and worthy of the followers of that sweet and omnipotent deity. The lover! no! he is not confounded with the herd of men, he does not degrade his soul, but elevates, drives on, and crowns it with light at the smile of the divinity. He becomes a supereminent being, and as such altogether incomprehensible. The universe—the vast universe, no longer capable of bounding his ideas, his affections, vanishes from before his sight. The soul of him who loves disdains restraint—nothing can restrain it. It launches itself out of the created, and creates in the infinite a world for itself, and for itself alone, how different from this obscure and fearful den!—is in the continued enjoyment of the sweetest ecstasy, is truly happy. All that has no relation to the object of its tenderness—all that is not that adored object, appears an insignificant point to his eyes. But where is he, susceptible of such love? Where? Who is capable of inspiring it? Oh love! I am all love. I cannot exist without love! My soul—my mortal fame—all my thoughts and affections, all that which I am, transfigures itself into one sole sentiment of love, and that sentiment will last eternally. Without love, life would become to me insupportable—the world an inhospitable and desolate desert, only haunted by spectres, so terrible to my sight, that to fly from them, I could cast myself into the mysterious but tranquil abode of death. Ah! yes! I prefer the sweet pains of love, the continual throbbing that accompany, the fear inseparable from it, to a to me stupid calm, and to all the pleasures that can supply the gratification of all other passions, all the goods (if without love there can be any good) which the world prizes and covets.

But how art thou profaned, O Love! What outrages do not the children of the earth commit in thy name divine! Often and often to affections the most illicit, to actions the most vile and degrading, to crime—ah! execrable iniquity! when even to crime itself they give the name of Love, and dare to tax it with the commission of crime! Alas! unheard-of blasphemy. Impious and sacrilegious that ye are, you not only feel it not, but comprehend not even what the word love signifies. Love has no wish but for virtue—Love inspires virtue—Love is the source of actions the most magnanimous, of true felicity—Love is a fire that burns and destroys not, a mixture of pleasure and of pain, a pain that brings pleasure, an essence eternal, spiritual, infinite, pure, celestial. This is the true, the only love—that sentiment which can alone entirely fill up the void of the soul—that horrible void, worse than death. Every other sentiment dissimilar from this, than this less pure, deserves not the sacred name of Love; and they who impiously profane and defile it, shall be punished by that most mighty of Divinities and shall merit eternal perdition. Where the soul that is feelingly alive seeks for love, and finds itself in the abyss of desolation, and where the heart is divested of this sweet fire, or finds faithless the object of its tenderness,—that miserable soul, let it seek (at least I so counsel it), let it seek, I say, its refuge in the tomb, and feed upon it and its last consolation."

This admirable piece of eloquence was perhaps the source of the inspiration of the *Epipsychidion*, a poem that combines the pathos of the Vita Nuova of Dante with the enthusiastic tenderness of Petrarch. The Epipsychidion is the apotheosis of love—Emilia a mere creature of his imagination, in whom he idealized Love in all its intensity of passion. His feeling toward the Psyche herself was, as may be seen by letter LX of his correspondence, a purely Platonic one. He calls the Epipsychidion a mystery, and says "as to real flesh and blood, you know that I do not deal in those articles. Expect nothing human or earthly from me," etc. His love for Emilia, if such it can in the general acceptation of the term be called, was of the kind described in the Symposium by Socrates.... Shelley thought that to pass from one state of existence to another, was not death, but a new development of life; that we must love as we live, through all eternity; and that they who have not this persuasion, know nothing of life, nothing of love; that they who do not make the universe a fountain whence they may literally draw new life and love, know nothing of one or the other, and are not fated to know anything of it. The words are not his, but they shadow out what I heard him better express.

This poem, or rhapsody, incomprehensible to the general class of readers, from a defect in the common organ of perception for the ideas of which it treats, fell dead from the press. I believe that not a copy of it was sold, not a single review noticed it—one of the many proofs that the public ear is deaf to the finest accords of the lyre.

Aphrodite-Venus is a figure in classical mythology altogether remote from the exalted Eros, I have spoken of.

Aphrodite is natural fruitfulness, or, Nature's productive power, hence the Romans identified the Greek Aphrodite with their own Venus, which was the goddess of Spring.

Only in the sense of "natural fruitfulness" is she a love goddess. She is rather a goddess of Beauty. Spring beautifies everything. When the later poets make Cupid (Amor) the son of Aphrodite, they understand no more by him Universal Love, but simply that passion, which natural beauty inspires.

The noblest conception one can get of Venus is the Venus Victrix, the victorious Venus, and Venus Urania, the heavenly Venus.

No paper about love is complete without saying something about Platonic love. I must therefore also say something. I will open the subject with a clipping from Scribner's Magazine, where a frivolous writer, under the heading, "The Point of View," says:

"Love between women and men was not invented for the entertainment of philosophers, but largely for domestic purposes; and if platonic love is to have anything better than a hazardous and unstable existence, the conditions of it must be such that it may prosper without conflict with Nature's more important ends. Thus we see why platonic friendships between young people who might marry do not endure. Such couples get married, and their friendship merges into a more durable sentiment, or else one of them marries someone else, and then it lapses. At least it should lapse, for if it does not, it not only militates against peace in a family, but it tends to keep the unmarried platonist from going about his business and finding himself a mate, according to Nature's design. It is true that there are women, and young women at that, who can contrive for a time to maintain a husband and one or two simultaneous platonic intimates. But in such cases one of three things happens: either the wife makes her husband happy and her platonic admirers miserable, or she makes her friends happy and her husband miserable, or she makes them all miserable. If by any chance or miracle of talent she seems to make them all happy, she makes society miserable, because it cannot see how she does it. And when society is miserable it talks, until finally it breaks up the arrangement. She is bound to fail, and the reason does not lie in any defect in her, but in the fact that her purpose is contrary to the economy of Nature, which has provided barely men enough to go around, and does not permit a woman who has a man of her own to monopolize other men with impunity. Every marriageable man besides her husband that any woman absorbs, involves the waste of some other woman's opportunities, and Nature abhors waste with a proverbial antipathy."

This is frivolity. This utilitarian writer is "away off." The sweet passion is unknown to him. The stories of Petrarch and Laura, Dante and Beatrice have no charm for him. His heart has not been "touched." The "beatific vision" has no meaning to him.

Let me answer his first lines by a little poem of Owen Meredith's:

> A poet loved a star,
> And to it whispered nightly:
> "Being so fair! why art thou love so far?
> Or why so coldly shine, who shinest so brightly?
> O Beauty woo'd and unpossessed,
> O might I to this beating breast
> But clasp thee once and then die blest."
>
> That star her poet's love,
> So wildly warm, made human.
> And leaving for his sake her heaven above,
> His star stoop'd earthward and became a woman.
> "Thou who hast woo'd and hast possessed,
> My lover, answer, which was best,
> The star's beam, or the woman's breast?"
>
> "I miss from heaven," the man replied,
> "A light that drew my spirit to it."
> And to the man the woman sigh'd,
> "I miss from earth a poet."

That's the answer to "the point of view," who has not taken the "point of view" correctly.

Whatever raptures *Venus vulgivata* may cause us, while we are young, we turn sooner or later from her and her gratifications and follow *Venus Urania*. When *Venus Urania*, the star, descends and becomes *Venus vulgivata*, we miss her from heaven. No light any more draws our Spirit upward.

*Venus vulgivata* and *Venus Urania* are the two poles of the same power. The one degrading. The other exalting. As in the magnetic bar, the middle is the point of indifference. We must profess the one or the other. Whichever we do worship for the time being, the opposite will cause a reaction and a healthy equilibrium. As in the magnet, our positive and negative forces will readjust themselves at once and find a new center. In this reaction and new equilibrium lies our salvation. This illustration contains the mystic key to all love.

It was an ancient Jewish custom of marriage for the wedded pair to drink from the same crystal cup and then break it in pieces. A wonderful symbol of love, active and transitoriness!

That custom also symbolized the frailty of earthly possessions and the transitiveness of earthly felicity. But, no matter how transitory, if the education remain after the cup has been dashed upon the earth, it is, after all as the Laureate sang:

> "Better to have loved and lost,
> Than never to have loved at all."

# QUESTIONS AND REMARKS.

The last meeting was given up to Questions and Remarks, some of which are here reproduced, together with other matter.

The Lecturer: It has been suggested that I should ask questions this afternoon rather than continue the subject of Nature-worship because, as I said, we ought to be outdoors for that subject. We can very well drop the subject now, for in a few months, in May or early in June, I am coming back. It has so been arranged. When I come back we will go into the country and study and worship together in the way we did at Greenacre last summer. Let me tell you how we did on one day, a day never to be forgotten by anybody who partook in the excursion to Mt. Salvat.

Some few of us arose with the sun and met him with greetings of joy on Observation Hill. Jehanghir Cola, the Parsee from Bombay, a true and real representative of fire worship, led the devotion. Facing the Sun, just as he had arisen above the horizon, Cola addressed to him the following hymn:

Praise be on thee, amplest of stars!
Revolving in the abundant love and greatness of God,
Abiding in the midst of perfect order,
Author of the powers of the senses,
Cause of whatever is produced anew, and creator of the seasons!
In the circle of thy sphere, which is without rent, which neither assumeth
A new shape nor putteth off an old one, nor taketh a straight course,
Thou, maker of the Day, art most near to the luster of God.
Thou art a symbol of his grandeur,
A beam of his glory;
Thou art as a proof of him upon his servants.
Clothing the stars with the garment of thy splendor.
Through the medium of thy active soul, which beameth with glory,
I seek him whose shadow thou art,—
The Lord that giveth harmony to worlds,
The Limit Establisher of all,
Light of lights!
That he may illuminate my soul with pure light, adorable knowledge,
    lofty excellence:
And make me one of those who are nigh unto him, who are filled with
    his love!

The newness of the experience, the solemnity of the occasion, never before partaken in by the majority of those present, the freshness of the morning and the glorious landscape in the early morning light, so thrilled them and all, that a new element entered their lives and controls them to this day. This world looked new. A new love, a new understanding, a new feeling had arisen. The occasion was so new and strange and the influence so powerful, that nobody said anything. Silently the company broke up and went home for breakfast.

At 9 a. m. the carriages were ready for those who wanted to drive, and the young started off on foot to Mt. Salvat, some carrying their lunches, others depending upon supplies sent over by wagon. In groups we walked over Observation Hill, through green fields and shady lanes, enjoying the magnificent scenery of the upper Piscataqua. You must not think that I am exaggerating in my description of the Greenacre scenery. I am not giving vent to subjective impressions. The Greenacre landscape is the only one, of the thousands I have seen in the various parts of the world, that has come near upsetting my philosophy. I have told you in the lectures of this course, that Nature is external mind and that mind is external Nature. I hold it to be so. I cannot see it to be otherwise. But at Greenacre I am an Aristotelian. There it seems to me that all things exist with a nature and characteristics of their own. These things communicate their nature and characteristics to me and I give them nothing. In the presence of that landscape I receive impressions which are a part of the landscape. I do not see beauty in the landscape; the landscape itself is beautiful. The aspect of it is part of its nature. I do not read "the father's face" into it, the landscape is idyllic, a little *eidullion*, "a little image." The first evening I spent at Greenacre, I watched the sun set from "Sunrise Camp," and it happened to me as it did to Wm. Blake, I did not see *with* my eyes, but *through* my eyes came to my soul the essence of that Golden Ball, and I heard it as "Glory to God on High"—"Peace on Earth"—"Good-will among Men." It was July 5th, 1896, never to be forgotten. It was a gorgeous sunset. All the heavens and the earth were still; the fleeting colors of roseate hues and ashen gray played in incalculable series of mutations. Behind the passing scenes, the glorious orb, incomparable emblem of Being, sank majestically down behind the distant White Hills, and before the scenes, as if in midair, I felt the Becoming. My reason could not arrest the movement, my understanding could not declare what it perceived. The glorious tints, the melting into one another, the lack of fixedness or duration, the deep, yet eloquent and sonorous silence spoke from Heaven and whispered

Eternal Harmony.

As I have said elsewhere, Greenacre is a revelation. The Great Being, self-luminous and self-reflected, lies upon the surface of everything at Greenacre. In the silksoft grass of the camp, the

"Kneippers" step upon the velvety garment of the great deity. The pebbles on the river shore are diamonds from his crown of glory. The weird nightly scenery and the magic around the Druid Stone bring you back to ages, when the gods wandered upon earth. When you rise from the cool waves of the Piscataqua, you rise out of the quiet place of your own soul, where the universe is reflected, and you are Anadyomene, infinite Love, begetting infinite Beauty.—There is God-communion and Nature—communion at Greenacre.

But, to return to my narrative.

When we arrived on Mt. Salvat and the various groups were gathered, I called them to order and sent the company divided in various divisions all over the hill. Some to study the northern sides of the trees and make observations on the relative growths, south and north; some were sent to observe the route the bees take back to their hive; some were to watch the flowers to see them turn after the sun; some were to read the formations of the clouds, etc. They were all to report at 2:30 what they had observed or discovered. While these observers were away, the young people had their "picnic" and the old their private naps or talks, or lunches. After all observations had been reported and notes made, most of the serious members of the company gathered with me in a shady place and I addressed them on the Father-influence of a mountain and told them how the sun is the civilizer of man. When the audience had realized their duty to worth-ship Father Sun, I asked them to arise, and, preserving the square in which they had been sitting, according to their color characteristics, to walk absolutely silently into an adjoining group of pines, there to assemble around a mighty stone found there. All walked triumphantly but silently into the wood and placed themselves as requested. In silence they all centered their thoughts upon the Sun. The occasion was solemn, the newness did not disturb any. When we had come to perfect rest around the stone we all joined hands in fellowship, and I addressed the universal powers, as far as I remember now, thus:

"Father Sun, great God of the universe, though Thou art not our God, we revere Thee, we worship Thee! Thou hast made us in the forms in which we now present ourselves before Thee! We thank Thee! This stone, around which we gather, is petrified life, once emanated from Thee! These trees, under whose shadow we stand and whose cool breezes refresh us and protect us against thy fiery darts, are also of Thee! In the presence of these universal witnesses we renew our allegiance to the Great, Good and Beautiful! Be Thou, O Sun a witness to our words; ye trees carry our message of heart-uplifts to all organic existence, and thou, stone, lie here upon this mountain till the end of days as an immovable tablet upon which we each for himself inscribe our vows!"

Involuntarily the audience burst out in the now famous Greenacre Uplift "Omnipresence manifest Thyself in me," and the emotion manifested was truly deep.

After a brief silence I called upon Dr. G. P. Wiksell to say something. Like an old Druid he stepped forward to the stone and renewed his vows. Cola came next and read a prayer from the Avesta.

The audience were as if spellbound. After a silence Miss Farmer started a final "Omnipresence," that seemed never to come to end, so deeply touched were all, and it repeated itself in all possible modulations and keys.

Not a word was said when we finally parted. Only this was remarked: "How singular; a pine cone lies on the very top of the stone!" In view of the lecture on the Pine cone which that audience had heard a few days ago, it was rather singular, that Nature for this occasion had provided a candle for our altar. Is anything singular?

In quietness and peace we all walked to the western slope of the hill to see the sun set. Ah! what a meaning that sunset had to all! Scattered around among the pines, the low-voiced prayer "Omnipresence" arose from all hearts, only interrupted by Cola's reading the same hymn to the sun, read in the morning. The singing continued till the sun had sunk 18 degrees below the horizon and the last roseate hues had turned gray. Then all arose and went home.

Next Spring, we will attempt to have a similar day somewhere in the neighborhood of Chicago.

Friends, excursions like the one described will do you more good than many lectures. You get dyspepsia and you have indigestion now from all the intellectual food you get. You get too much of it.

Before bidding you "Good Bye" or rather *au revoir* I wish to say a word or two about the way you should look upon that which I have said. I have not attempted to instruct you, I have rather spoken personally. I have let myself be open to you and have given experiences. I have tried to speak from that fourth plane, I spoke of in my first address. In thus giving expression to my feelings, sensations and perceptions, I have laid myself open to many criticisms, I know. But I have trusted myself to you and do so now in going away. I have done this because I wish that you in the future would ask all your lecturers to do likewise. Make them be personal. Let them give their own experiences and not something they have read in books and only poorly digested. Even initiations, as now understood, are no warrant for the truth. You can not be sure of the life there is in a teaching, unless it is given you by one who has lived it, by one who teaches from experiences and thus vouches for the teaching. The teacher must trust you and you must trust the teacher. In soul life no abstract teachings are worth much. We learn and we teach by *Presence*. The spell of presence is the ideal education. If you want learning and nothing else, go to the books, and you can go there alone. But if you want education, viz., to be brought out of yourself and into your highest Self, you want the loving presence of a companion, a fellow pilgrim. Hereafter, call only fellow-pilgrims to lecture to you. Living power begets living convictions, and convictions move the world. Only by such methods will your Ministry be a ministry and a blessing.

Au revoir till Spring! May the Blessing of the Great Love be upon us all.

# APPENDIX TO LECTURES ON NATURE-WORSHIP.

We have heard so much about "the order of nature," "law of nature," etc., as applied to morals and society, that I think I do you a favor by reprinting the most interesting part of the famous Volney's "The Law of Nature," which was a catechism for French citizens.

Q. What is the law of Nature?

A. It is the constant and regular order of action by which God governs the universe; an order which his wisdom presents to the senses and to the reason of men, as an equal and common rule for their actions, to guide them, without distinction of country or of sect, toward perfection and happiness.

Q. Do such orders exist in Nature? What does the word nature signify?

A. The word nature bears three different senses:

1st, It signifies the universe, the material world; in this first sense they say, "the beauty of Nature, the richness of Nature;" i. e., the objects in the heavens and on the earth exposed to our sight.

2dly, It signifies the power that animates, that moves the universe, considering it as a distinct being, such as the soul is to the body. In this second sense they say, "the intentions of Nature, the incomprehensible secrets of Nature."

3dly, It signifies the operations of that power on each being, or on each class of beings; and in this third sense they say, the nature of man is an enigma; every being acts according to its nature.

Wherefore, as the actions of each being, or of each species of beings are subjected to constant and general rules, which cannot be infringed without interrupting and troubling the general or particular order, those rules of actions and of motions are called the natural laws, or laws of Nature.

Q. What are the characters of the law of Nature?

A. There can be assigned ten principal ones.

Q. Which is the first?

A. To be inherent to the existence of things, and consequently primitive and anterior to every other law; so that all those which men have received, are only imitations of it, and their perfection is ascertained by the resemblance they bear to this primordial model.

Q. Which is the second?

A. To be derived immediately from God to be presented by him to each man; whereas all other laws are presented to us by men, who may be either deceived, or deceivers.

Q. Which is the third?

A. To be common to all times, and to all countries: that is to say, one and universal.

Q. Is no other law universal?

A. No: for no other law is agreeable, or applicable to all the people of the earth; all of them are local and accidental, originating from circumstances of places and of persons; so that if such a man had not existed, such an event had not taken place—such a law would never have been made.

Q. Which is the fourth character?

A. To be uniform and invariable.

Q. Is no other law uniform and invariable?

A. No: for what is good and virtue according to one, is evil and vice according to another; and what one and the same law approves of at one time, it often condemns afterwards.

Q. Which is the fifth character?

A. To be evident and palpable, because it consists entirely of facts incessantly present to the senses, and to demonstration.

Q. Are not other laws evident?

A. No: for they are founded on past and doubtful facts, on equivocal and suspicious testimonies, and on proofs inaccessible to the senses.

Q. Which is the sixth character?

A. To be reasonable, because its precepts and entire doctrine are conformable to reason, and to the human understanding.

Q. Is no other law reasonable?

A. No: for all are in contradiction to the reason and the understanding of men, and tyrannically impose on him a blind and impracticable belief.

Q. Which is the seventh character?

A. To be just, because in that law, the penalties are proportionate to the infractions.

Q. Are not other laws just?

A. No: for they often exceed bounds, either in rewarding deserts, or in punishing delinquencies; and they often impute to meritorious, or criminal intentions, null or indifferent actions.

Q. Which is the eighth character?

A. To be pacific and tolerant, because in the law of nature, all men being brothers, and equal in rights, it recommends to them, peace and toleration, even for errors.

Q. Are not other laws pacific?
A. No: for all preach dissension, discord, and war; and divide mankind by exclusive pretensions of truth and domination.
Q. Which is the ninth character?
A. To be equally beneficent to all men, in teaching them the true means of becoming better and happier.
Q. Are not other laws beneficent likewise?
A. No: for not one of them teaches the means of attaining happiness—all are confined to pernicious and futile practices: this is evident from facts, since, after so many laws, so many religions, so many legislators and prophets, men are still as unhappy and as ignorant as they were five thousand years back.
Q. Which is the last character of the law of Nature?
A. That it is alone sufficient to render men happier and better, because it contains all that is good and useful in other laws, either civil or religious; that is to say, it constitutes essentially the moral part of them; so that if other laws were divested of it, they would be reduced to chimerical and imaginary opinions, devoid of any practical utility.
Q. How do our sensations deceive us?
A. In two ways: by ignorance, and by passion.
Q. When do they deceive us by ignorance?
A. When we act without knowing the action and effect of objects on our senses: for example, when a man touches nettles without knowing their stinging quality, or when he swallows opium without knowing its soporiferous effect.
Q. When do they deceive us by passion?
A. When, conscious of the pernicious action of objects, we abandon ourselves, notwithstanding, to the impetuosity of our desires, and of our appetites: for example, when a man who knows that wine intoxicates, does nevertheless drink it to excess.
Q. What is good according to the law of Nature?
A. It is everything that tends to preserve and perfect man.
Q. What is evil?
A. It is everything that tends to spoil or destroy man.
Q. Which are the individual virtues?
A. They are five principal ones in number:
1st, Science, which comprises prudence and wisdom.
2dly, Temperance, which comprises sobriety and chastity.
3dly, Courage, or strength of body, and of the soul.
4thly, Activity; that is to say, the love of labor, and the employment of time; and in short, cleanliness or purity of body, as well in dress as in habitation.
Q. How does the law of Nature prescribe science?
A. By the reason that man, who knows the causes and effects of things, attends in an extensive and sure manner to his preserva-

tion, and to the development of his faculties. Science is to him the eye and the light that enables him to discern clearly, and with justness, the objects amidst which he moves; and hence the word enlightened man is made use of, to signify a learned and instructed man. Science and instruction furnish us, unfailingly, with resources and means of subsisting; and this is what prompted a philosopher that was shipwrecked to say, in the midst of his companions, who were lamenting bitterly the loss of their wealth, "for my part, I carry all my wealth within me."

Q. Which is the vice contrary to science?
A. It is ignorance.
Q. How does the law of Nature forbid ignorance?
A. By the grievous detriments which result from it to our existence; for the ignorant man, who knows neither causes nor effects, commits, every instant, errors the most pernicious, both to himself and to others; he resembles a blind man, who gropes his way at random, and runs, or is run against, by every one he meets.
Q. What is temperance?
A. It is a regular use of our faculties, which makes us never exceed, in our sensations, the end of Nature to preserve us: it is the moderation of passions.
Q. Which is the vice contrary to temperance?
A. The disorder of the passions, the avidity of all kind of enjoyments; in a word, cupidity.
Q. Which are the principal branches of temperance?
A. Sobriety, continence, or chastity.
Q. Does the law of Nature forbid the use of certain kinds of meat, or of certain vegetables, on particular days, during certain seasons?
A. No: it absolutely forbids, only whatever is injurious to health; its precepts, in this respect, vary according to persons, and they constitute a very delicate and important science; for the quality, the quantity, and the combination of ailments have the greatest influence, not only over the momentary affections of the soul, but even over its habitual disposition. A man is not the same fasting as after a meal; even were he sober, a glass of spirituous liquor, or a dish of coffee, give degrees of vivacity, of mobility, of disposition to anger, sadness, or gaiety; such a meat, because it lies heavy on the stomach, engenders moroseness and melancholy; such another, because it assists digestion, creates sprightliness, and an inclination to oblige and to love. The use of vegetables, because they have little nourishment, renders the body weak, and gives a disposition to repose, idleness, and ease. The use of meat, because it is full of nourishment, stimulates the nerves, and therefore gives vivacity, uneasiness, and audacity. Now from those habitudes of ailment result habits of constitution and of the

organs, which form at length different kinds of temperaments, distinguishing each by a peculiar characteristic. And it is for this reason that, in hot countries especially, legislators have made laws respecting regimen or food. The ancients were taught by long experience, that the dietic science constituted a great part of the moral science. Amongst the Egyptians, the ancient Persians, and even amongst the Greeks, at the areopagus, important affairs were examined fasting. And it has been remarked, that amongst those people, where public affairs were discussed during the heat of meals, and the fumes of digestion, deliberations were hasty and turbulent, and the results of them frequently unreasonable, and productive of turbulence and disturbance.

Q. Does the law of Nature prescribe continence?

A. Yes: because a moderate use of the most lively of pleasures is not only useful, but indispensable, to the support of strength and health; and because a simple calculation proves, that for some minutes of privation, you increase the number of your days, both in vigor of body and of mind.

Q. How does it forbid libertinism?

A. By the numerous evils which result from it to the physical and the moral existence.

Q. Are courage, and strength of body and mind virtues in the law of Nature?

A. Yes; and most important virtues; they are the efficacious and indispensable means of attending to our preservation and welfare. The courageous and strong man repulses oppression, defends his life, his liberty, and his property. By his labor he procures himself an abundant subsistence, which he enjoys in tranquillity and peace of mind. If he fails under misfortunes, from which his prudence could not protect him, he supports them with firmness and resignation; and it is for this reason that the ancient moralists have placed strength and courage on the list of the four principal virtues.

Q. Should weakness and cowardice be considered as Vices?

A. Yes; since it is certain that they produce innumerable calamities.

Q. Are idleness and sloth vices in the law of Nature?

A. Yes, and the most pernicious of all vices; for they lead to every other.

Q. Why do you place cleanliness in the ranks of virtues?

A. Because it is, in reality, one of the most important amongst them, on account of its powerful influence over the health and preservation of the body. Cleanliness, as well in dress as in residence, obviates the pernicious effects of the humidity, the baneful odors, and contagious exhalations, which exhale from all things abandoned to putrefaction: cleanliness maintains free transpiration; it renews the air, refreshes the blood, and disposes even the mind to alacrity.

From this it appears, that persons attentive to the cleanliness of their body and habitations, are, in general, more healthy, and less exposed to distempers, than those who live in the midst of filth and nastiness; again, it is further remarked, that cleanliness carries along with it throughout all the branches of domestic administration, habits of order and arrangement, which is one of the first means and first elements of happiness.

Q. Uncleanliness, or filthiness, is therefore a real vice?

A. Yes, as real a one as drunkenness or idleness from which, in a great measure, it is derived.

Q. Does the law of Nature order sincerity?

A. Yes; for lying, perfidy, and perjury creates distrust, quarrels, hatred, revenge, and a crowd of evils amongst men, which tends to their common destruction; whilst sincerity and fidelity establish confidence, concord, and peace, besides the infinite good resulting from such a state of things to society.

All wisdom, all perfection, all law, all virtue, all philosophy, consist in the practice of those axioms founded on our own organization,

> PRESERVE THYSELF;
> INSTRUCT THYSELF;
> MODERATE THYSELF;

Live for thy fellow citizens—that they may live for thee.

# APPENDIX TO LECTURE ON LOVE.

The unfortunate Algernon Sidney was born 1622 and beheaded 1683. His essay on love has been very rare and was in our day only reprinted once in "Nineteenth Century," 1884.

### ALGERNON SIDNEY ON LOVE.

Love is the passion that hath passed all censures, as various as the kinds of it, or the effects. It is by all esteemed the most powerful of passions, by most the best; some stick not to say it is the worst, because the least controuleable by reason. It is of as many kinds as theare are objects in the world, and inclinations in men: but I intend at this time only to speake of that to beauty, the height of which we commonly call being in love. This consists of as many sorts as beauty, which are two, that of the mind, and that of the boddy; the Platonicks adde a thirde, which is of sounds, and if anything may be called beauty that hath proportion and correspondence of parts, that name may certainly agree with sounds, though they are to be judged neither by the eye, nor the understanding, which are generally esteemed the powers that distinguish betwixt beauty and deformity; but, howsoever, theis tow only will fall under my discourse, for what excellence soever is in sounds, that can only be an invitation, and not the object of love, unlesse a man could be fancied to be nothing but eare, as eccho is nothing but voice, (that is to say) nothing at all, and so incapable of anything, or of being. The Stoicks, generall enemyes to all passions, doe also reject this, as that which doth toe much soften the mind, depriving it theareby of that firmenesse of temper, which is that only in which reason delights and governes; never the lesse storyes are full of thoes wise men whoe for all theire pretended austerity have fallen as deeply under the power of that passion as any other in the world, as if the Divine Power had made use of it to shew them the vanitye of theire principles. Epicureans allow soe much of it as conduceth to pleasure, but reject the transporting part; and to shew how well they make this good, Lucretius, one of the cheife fathers of that sect, for all his philosophy grew soe desperately in love with a young wench, who rejecting him for his old age, he in rage threw himself downe a steep rock into the sea. But the Platonicks are the perfect patrons of that passion, even to the degree of disliking hardly anything that carryes that name.

Love is the most intense desire of the soule to enjoy beauty, and wheare it is reciprocal, is the most entire and exact union of harts. Divers reasons are given for the birth and groweth of it; some esteeme likenesse of natures, others like constellations ruling at the time of birth. For my owne part I can only conclude, that whatsoever pleaseth the eye and the fancye is beautifull, whatsoever we think beautifull we desire to enjoy, and that desire is love. Theare is also tow kinds of this love, the one perfectly spiritual which is called the celestial Venus, and having its seat only in the minde hathe the mind only for its object, delights in virtue and excellence of understanding, neglects the visible beauty, contents itself solely with that fruition which is to be had by conversation. The other is absolutely sensuall, makes the exterior part its object, and hath no other end than sensuall pleasure: the first is an affection for Angells, pure and contemplative, the other for beasts, filthy and sottish.

Man is a creature composed of both theis, a celestiall and angellicall part, which is the soule, and of the terrestriall, fleshy, bestiall part, which is his boddy, soe that his affections ought to participate of both his natures, rejecting that which solely consists in the admiration of the soule, as that which he can very imperfectly judge of, and where the knowledge is imperfect, the desire must needs be very cold. Neither is he pleased with the other; thoes are but weak chaines which take hold only of our senses: the principall part in us challengeth a share in all our pleasures, and must have wheare with all to content itself or else there is nothing fixed. Therefore a man, to love as a man, must have regard to both; and as long as he is in any degree reasonable, can fix his hart neither absolutely uppon that which is too high to be understood, nor too low to be approved: a mixed creature must have mixed affections, and can love only wheare he finds a mind of such excellency as to delight his understanding, and a body of beauty to please his senses: and the mind being by much the most considerable part in us, the principal care is for the pleasing of that; for the mind being the only fixed power in us, fixed affections can only grow from thence. The eyes are wandering, the senses uncertaine, the desires that proceed from them must be soe allsoe; the necessity of which appears in this: everything acts according to a principle within itself. An Angell loves spiritually; a beast, that is all flesh, comprehends not spiritual things any more than an Angell tasts carnal things, and a man that is composed of reason and sense, rationally and sensually both together. Besides, every agent proposeth to itself enjoyment of good, (that is pleasure) for all that is good is pleasant and nothing ought to please but that which is good; that is good only that satisfyes; that can never satisfye, which is agreeable only to one part of a composed creature. The soule disdains sensuall pleasures; the senses taste not the spirituall, so that to please both the object must be such as both may joyne in the enjoyment.

I will conclude this point with this assertion; the spirituall affections are soe cold as hardly to have any being; sensuall are soe madde as to be unworthy of anything that pretends to a reasonable soule; and the strong, lasting, high, and perfectly humane passions, are only those which proceed from the admonition of an excellent mind clothed with a beautiful boddy. This is a rare jewel well set, and fit to be sought after with all the powers of the soule and boddy, as that only which can content both with the fullest and most absolute happinesse that our natures can be capable of, in comparison of which all other worldly pleasures are vaine and empty shadows, unworthy of being sought with intention of mind or enjoyed with any satisfaction. Happy therefore is he who hath his hopes and desires crowned with successe, or that in the search of them being denied pleasure in life, finds ease and rest in death.

To this I may add, that everything is received according to the measure of the receiver, and every man loves more or lesse spiritually or sensually, as he doth more approach to the angelicall or bestiall nature; for the same degrees and differences that are in our persons are allsoe in our affections, and though it be true that some love as sensually as beasts, yet will it not follow that others attaine to the spirittuality of Angels; for it is very ordinary to see thoes that have the shapes of men so absolutely corrupted with vice, that they seem to have no soule, or so much as serves them instead of salt only, to keep them from corrupting and stinking; but the other sort is not seene amongst men, I meane thoes of angellicall perfections. The best of men are troubled with frailetyes and vices, the worst have nothing else; for which noe other reason perhaps can be given, then that it is soe seemed good to the Divine Wisdom; unlesse you will take this for one, that we have within ourselves a power of doing or being ill, but that our recovery from that condition of illnesse which is natural to us, is by the power of God upon our harts, whoe gives his graces unto such men, at such times, and in such proportion as he pleaseth, leaving us still with many infirmityes, that we may humble ourselves, and acknowledging God to be the Author of all good, depend upon him for a delivery from all interior and exterior ills; and reserves the state of perfection to fill up the measure of our happinesse, when we come to that of immortality. To this I may adde that morally vice is easy and naturall to us, but virtue is to be understood only by discourse, and practised by care; into the first every foole can runne blindfold, the other is only the work of an excellent spirit, refined by great maturity and strength of wisdome; to the one facility invites, from the other difficulty deters, which is as much more eminent in the one then the other, as it is harder for one that is placed in the middest of a steepe rock, to climbe up to the top thereof, then to throw himself downe to the bottome.

The next point is to shew what is the strength and power of this affection. It is generally concluded by all to be the strongest of all, and besides what every man that hath tasted of it finds within his owne brest, all books are full of storyes of such as have in comparison of the person loved, despised all worldly things, and being possessed by that passion, bin transported to actions much beyond theire ordinary facultyes, either good or ill, as the nature of the persons affection or the present occasion inclined and required. But all that is alleaged by others is cold and weake in comparaison of what thoes find within theire owne harts whoe have bin capable of this best and noblest of passions. Theire whole mind is full of but one thought: the allurements of the world, which other men call pleasures, they have no tast of; the businesse is tedious and insupportable; theire whole care and industry is solely imployed in serving and pleasing the beloved person. They are strangers to feare, joy, greife, hope, anger, but such as spring from love. Theire desires are most intensively placed upon one object, which by a strange violence transports us beyond our selves, gives courage to the most fearfull, sharpens the wit of the most simple, gives felicity to the most depraved minds, constancy to the most unsettled, and of itself alone hath power to draw thoes harts which have received it to acts of goodnesse, honesty, virtue, and gallantry, with more efficacy then all the most exact examples of history, and precepts of phylosophy.

The reason of this I take to be, that love for its end proposeth the enjoyment of beauty; beauty consists in order, harmony, and uniformity, unto which all ill actions have an absolute contrariety, having neither rule, order, forme, or measure, but are like vice, the spring from whence they flow, full of confusednesse and deformity. Besides, he that loves desires to render himself acceptable to the person loved, which being full of virtuous inclinations, (or at least thought to be soe by the lover) doth abhorre all that is not agreeable to reason and goodnesse, and the lover finding nothing to be pleasing but that which is suitable to the affections of the object of his passion, rejects and hates all depraved desires as destructive to his chiefe designe, and thearefore with an active earnestnesse applyes himself to correct the defects of his owne nature, which hath produced more excellent actions then all the affections in the world put together; unlesse I am mistaken in this, that it is not love that makes them virtuous, but being virtuous inclines them to love.

But least that by proposing the enjoyment of beauty for the end of love, I should be too much drowned in sensuallity, I must explain myself a littell. It is very certaine that all desire is for fruition; but that fruition that satisfyes a desire must be of the same nature with the desire itself. Sensuall desires are satisfyed with sensuall fruition, spirituall with spirituall, mixt with mixt; or that I may not trouble myself with tearms, I may in one word comprehend all, the desire of a lover to be loved, and that perfect union of hearts is the perfection of lovers happinesse; for though we are inclinable to desire the senses may not be excluded, yet having the principal end of our desires, wee may rest fully satisfied, tho' that in some particulars wee find ourselves crossed by fortune; for he cannot be said to want any thing that is made one with the person that is full of all excellencies. Neither is it extravagant for mee whoe professe love to beauty to be contented with spirituall fruition; for though in my choice I aime at the beauty of the boddy, it is principally theareby to discover the beauty of the mind; for nature, which delights in proportion, suites not an excellent mind with a deformed boddy, nor a vicious (that is deformed) mind in a beautifull boddy. Nature's works are not like hippocrites or sepulchers, beautiful without and rottenesse within. It weare a deceipt to cover the wretched wickednesse of a vicious mind with thoes glorious ornaments of beauty which make up one of the attributes of the Deity; and whereas beauty, which is the greatest excellency of things created as well as uncreated, and is in things created a motive to us to admire the greatnesse and goodnesse of the Creator, if it did palliate vice, would be the greatest snare to us that is imaginable, and instead of delighting in the outward resemblance of God, bring us to worship the Devill. But an intention to deceave our weake natures cannot proceed from the spirit of goodnesse; that is a diamond set in gold, and the other a worthlesse flint, which he suffers to ly in the dirt.

That is truely excellent, which God hath caused to shine with the glory of his own rayes; wheare soever theire is beauty I can never doubt of goodnesse.

Thoes parts of the sea that are safe have calm and smoth waters, but wheare dangerous rocks lye at the bottome, even the surface is perpetually rough and troubled. It is true that not only age impaires all beautyes, but many are destroyed by accidents, from which even the most excellent are not exempted, as the safest parts of the sea may be disturbed and troubled with storms; but that opposeth not my pourpose, for ayming at reall, not phantasticall excellence, I look for the naturall, not the accidentall beauty or deformity, and will noe more grant that a beautifull face can by the small pox or any other accident grow deformed to one that knew and loved it before, then that a deformed can change its nature by painting, though both will deceave any eyes that have not excellent facultyes of decerning.

Upon all which it will appear, that the beautye of the boddy gives the beginning to love, but that after the image thereof is graven upon a hart, and the beautye of the mind discovered, it is not in the power of age, or any naturall or accidentall cause to roote it out or deface it; for that which at the first was only the act of the fancy by the help of the eye, is now growne to be the act of the understanding firmly fixed in the hart and mind, which being the governing power in man, finding its own desires satisfied in being loved, finds rest within itself; and though theare is a flame remayning in the senses, which mutiny for theare part alsoe of fruition they are not able to cause any great disturbance in a man that is reasonable. But if the mind faile of its desire, the whole frame of man is in confusion, the hart is rent asunder by the violence of passion, and theare is noe power left to appease the rage of the senses. This extremity of disorder and torment seems fabulous to thoes that have not felt it within themselves; every one is apt to say, if he cannot obtain the affections of one person, why doth he not apply his to another who is more kind? But they littell understand love's mystery who use theis discourses, for noe man is in love but with an opinion of the excellency of the beloved person above all others, and hath absolutely resigned his hart unto hir. The most exact beautyes seeme but vaine shaddowes, the excellentest minds but imperfect images of hir imperfection; and failing of his desire in enjoying hir only who hath the power of his hart, despiseth all things else; and being despised by her, hates all that himself despiseth.

And that which fills up the measure of the rejected lover's torment, is, that despaire will not cure it, for to love without hope is but a seeming contradiction; for though hope is to desire as fuel is to fire, the elementary fire burnes without the fuel, and passion grounded upon confession of excellence outlives hope. Or if theare be such a power of man to confine his desires to his hope (which I believe only in thoes that are weake, faint and grounded only upon some trifling convenience) they are of all men most happy, theire calme brests are free from disorder, and while other wretches are in trouble, they find perfect peace, their love serves only to procure pleasure, and like a strong well-tempered stomach, either drawes nourishment out of whatsoever it receaves or casts it up; soe they trye all, and retaine only such as encrease their happinesse.

Neverthelesse a true and perfect lover would not procure his owne rest, by defacing the beloved image which with soe much joye he printed in his owne hart; but I think this part of discourse is frivoulous as impossible, and that same image doth take such root, and growes soe entirely one with the hart, that both must live and die together without possibility of separation. At least with me I am sure it is; my passion hath made itself master of all the facultyes of my mind, and hath destroyed all that is in opposition unto it; I live in it, and by it; it is all that I am; take away that and I am nothing. I can neither conforme my desires to my hopes, nor raise my hopes to my desires; the lownesse and meannesse of my fortune and person forbids me to hope; the beautye and lovelinesse of the person whome I love makes my desires approach as neare to eternity, as that can doe which is seated in a mortal foundation. My constancy is both my fault and my punishment; death only can give me a dismission from either.

Having spoken something of what love is, and of the effects of it, it is now time to see wheather it ought to be reproved or commended, denied the entrance into harts, turned out, or embraced; or rather if I had observed any methode, when I spoke something of others opinions upon it, should have finished my owne, but I writing only to day that which I shall reade the next week or moneth, and then burne, having noe other intention but to ease my troubled thoughts, and to attaine to the knowledge of myself, by setting down naifely the true state of my mind, I littell care for thoes rules which are necessary to thoes whoe are to depend on others judgements, I content myself with setting downe my thoughts, without caring for rule or order, as appears by breaking and returning to my story; by affirming first that one of the principall works for which we are sent into this world, is to admire the works of him that made both us and it; thoes are the most excellent that are the most beautifull (for beauty is the perfection of excellence) and those works of nature are of the most perfect beauty, which are living, and of the living, the reasonable only can content a reasonable soule: the most excellent therefore in beauty of reasonable creatures, doth best deserve our admiration, and theareby we do fulfill a great part of the end for which we were created. But who can admire any thing without desiring the fruition of it, and that desire is love.

For what reason can be imagined for the difference that we see in persons, (for the same power that made all things could have made all alike perfect) but to make theareby a difference in our affections towards them? Why are some made glorious in beauty but to draw the affections unto them? Why others cursed with deformity, but to give the greater luster unto thoes that are contrary to them, or to shew the illnesse of their natures, as marks that men should beware of them? How blind a sottishnesse, is it, not to see and distinguish of beauty, and what a beastly malice it is not to love that which we acknowledge to be excellent! The glory of divine rayes doe appeare in faces, but much more in minds;

whoe can then without barbarity (I think I may say impiety) deny to suffer himself to be ravished with the admiration of such an excellence of a created beauty, as is an image of the uncreateh, or to be inflamed with the love of it, and the desire to enjoy it? If desires weare absolutely sinfull, they had never bin given us; if beauty might not be desired, it had never been created: theare is noe forbidden fruite out of Paradice. We have a free liberty of enjoying all that is good: goodnesse and beauty are convertible tearmes and indivisible things, and they are happy that attaine unto it: they that are wise desire that which is best.

But some will say, we ought to desire even the best things with moderation, which love destroyes: Ah! let that extend to ordinary things—Desire riches, honours and the like coldly, and unpassionately: they cannot content the mind, thearefore ought not to possesse it, but wheare beauty of mind and boddy meet, both in such excellency as leave not liberty to the fancy to imagine any thing more perfect, whoe can attribute too much either to it or the Author, since that alone is able fully to satisfy all our desires? Worldly things doe often cloy us, but never content us. Some consist wholly in contemplation, entertain the mind, neglect or destroy the boddy; others that satisfy the senses, distast the mind, perhaps hurt it: but such of our pleasure have their worth only from our vanity; but this, a Person soe qualified leaves noe part of us unsatisfied, nor any thing in relation to this world to be wished to compleat our happinesse; weare it not then much better to use that prudence by which they pretend to moderate theire affections, only in making choice of such a person to be the object of them, as may absolutely deserve their utmost intentions?

Besides what can reasonably be brought to fortify this opinion, if we examine what men have bin free or possessed with this passion, we shall find few that have not tasted of it, unlesse they be ordinary and vulgar spirits, or such as by the vanity of ambition or some other furious passion or vice (which love abhorres) transported even into madnesse, which neverthelesse hathe not defended some of them from being made slaves to Venus. And amongst the heathens, the Poets whoe weare theare wisest men, and in their fables comprehended all the misteryes of phylosophy, exempted not theire gods from this passion. And amongst Christians, I know but tow cautions that are but by men of understanding, which are, that love to the creature be not of such a degree as to take us from the worship and love of God; th' other that we defend ourselves from unlawful desires, both of which I grant, and yet have as much as I desire; for that same love, for which God created and beautified the world, is the only means for us to returne unto him, who is the fountain of our being: and through the imperfections of our owne natures being not able to see or comprehend his greatnesse and goodnesse otherwise then by his works, must make us from visible things to raise our thoughts up to him. And for unlawful desires, they are not more contrary unto religion then to love, which delights only in beauty and virtue, hates the deformity of vice, and of that brutish lust which distinguisheth not of honour or justice. He cannot be said to love a woman, that would buy his owne pleasure with hir dishonour or crime; he only loves himself. Besides, the love which I defend being in a great degree spirituall, cannot desire any thing that is vicious; vice destroys the principall object of love (which is the mind) and the benefite that is reaped by such pleasures, can only satisfy the senses, which thearefore love not only desires not, but hates.

But the greatest reason why we should apply ourselves to oppose the birth and growth of this passion, is the infinite paines and sorrowes that it causeth, how many are made miserable for one that attaines to happinesse by it; and even thoes are first exposed to all miseries before they obtaine theare desire. And truly to this I have very littell to answeare; only this, that as love is the cause of the greatest ills that men suffer, it is the cause alsoe of the most perfect pleasures, consisting only in extreams, and as many are made miserably by love, none are made happy without love. It is the most active instrument of our natures, and causeth the most good or hurt to us. But though a quiet indifferent state, voide of great griefes or joyes, weare to be chosen rather then this slippery precipice, from whence we are soe likely to fall into misery, discourses upon it weare vaine; for our weak reason, which should be our guide, is carried away captive by the power of beauty and virtue, against which blindnesse only and stupidity are able to make any defence.

Theare is another sort of people whoe are great pretenders to wisdome, whoe say that the objects of our desires should be such as satisfy the mind, and that if any such can be found, too great a valeu cannot be put upon it, but deny that can be found amongst women; they are only light creatures, fit to satisfy the senses, maintain our species, and quensh our naturall desires, and have not such mindes as can give delight to a wise man.

How great an ignorance is this! Socrates learnt his phylosophy from Pictinna: though shee receaved hir first principles from him, shee grew soe excellent as to be able to teach hir master, whoe was able to teach all the rest of the world. And Pericles, to whome all Greece gave the preference for wisdome, confessed he knew nothing but what he had learnt from the faire Aspasia; both of which weare as excellent for their beauty as understanding: and whoe is it that doth not know that every age hath produced some very excellent in thoes things for which men most prize themselves, and yet theis grave fooles despise them?

It is true that weomen have not thoes helps from studdy and education as men have, but in the natural powers of the mind are noe ways inferior. They exempt themselves from the trouble of thoes knotty sciences that serve only to deceave fooles, which furnish the tongue with wordes, but tend nothing to the framing of the understanding; and instead of this they have a pleasantnesse of wit in conversation very much beyond men, and a well composednesse of judgment, which, if they did not deserve our love, would move our envy: and unto whatsoever they apply themselves, either learning, businesse, domestick or publike governement, shew themselves at the least equall to our sex. I should be glad if I could except military business, naturally disliking any thing of violence amongst them: but even in that many have bin excellent.

But above all, the softnesse, gentlenesse, and sweetnesse that is in them, doth justly move our love and admiration, whereas mens minds are as ruggid and harsh as theire faces; fit for boisterous action by the strength and hardinesse of theire boddyes, but incapable of giving pleasure: and even in that quality which men soe much prize in themselves, which is courage, how many of them hath been faine to take example in generous and bold resolutions from theire wives, daughters, or mistresses. Epicharis suffered torture better than any of forty the most eminent senators of Rome, of divers kindred of the chiefe of the soldiery, concealing by hir constancy the conspiracy which the weaknesse of the others revealed. Seneca was glad to receave encouragement and example to dye from Paulina, Petus from Arria in his extremity, and the famous Brutus often from Porcia: besides infinite number of exemples of virtue, by which that sweet sexe shewes they can, when it is needfull, excell ours in gallantry as well as beauty, and gives us sufficient reason to conclude that they cannot only mitigate the troubles of our life, which wee through a turbelent illnesse of nature create to one another, but by theire examples mollify our hardinesse by pleasures we receave from them, recompense the mischief our harsh tempers expose us unto, and that they only are the worthy objects of our affections, it being as evident that we owe our pleasures to them, as our birth; they are only to ease our griefs and cares, and which is more beneficiall unto us, soften that rigid fiercenesse of mind which is our crime and plague, the instruments of our owne and others miseryes, by the sweet allurements of pleasure that we receave from them; let not any man through a fond and impudent presumption in his owne merit despise that sex.

# EPILOGUE.

"Should I be visited by corporeal suffering, pain, or disease, I cannot avoid *feeling* them, for they are accidents of my nature; and, as long as I remain here below I am a part of Nature. But they shall not *grieve* me. They can only touch the nature with which in a wonderful manner I am united,—not myself, the being exalted above all Nature. The sure end of all pain, and of all sensibility to pain, is death; and of all things which the mere natural man is wont to regard, as evils, this is to me the least. I shall not die to myself, but only to others; to those who remain behind, from whose fellowship I am torn:—for myself the hour of Death is the hour of Birth to a new, more excellent life.

"Now that my heart is closed against all desire for earthly things, now that I have no longer any sense for the transitory and perishable, the universe appears before my eyes clothed in a more glorious form. The dead inert mass, which only filled up space, has vanished; and in its place there flows onward, with the rushing music of mighty waves, an endless stream of life and power and action, which issues from the original Source of all life—from Thy Life, O Infinite One! for all life is Thy Life, and only the religious eye penetrates to the realm of True Beauty.

"I am related to Thee, and all that I behold around me is related to me; all is life and soul, and regards me with bright spirit-eyes, and speaks with spirit-voices to my heart. In all the forms that surround me, I behold the reflection of my own being broken up into countless diversified shapes, as the morning sun, broken in a thousand dew-drops, throws back its splendors to itself.

"Thy Life, as alone the finite mind can conceive it, is self-forming, self-manifesting Will:—this Life, clothed to the eye of the mortal with manifold sensible forms, flows forth through me, and throughout the immeasurable universe of Nature. Here it streams as self-creating and self-forming matter through the veins and muscles, and pours out its abundance into the tree, the plant, the grass. Creative life flows forth in one continuous stream, drop on drop, through all forms, and places where my eye can follow it; it reveals itself to me, in a different shape in each various corner of the universe, as the same power by which in secret darkness my own frame was formed. There, in free play, it leaps and dances as spontaneous activity in the animal, and manifests itself in each new form as a new, peculiar, self-subsisting world; the same power which, invisibly to me, moves and animates my own frame. Everything that lives and moves follows this universal impulse, this one principle of all motion, which, from one end of the universe to the other, guides the harmonious movement;—in the animal *without freedom;* in me, from whom in the visible world the motion proceeds, although it had not its source in me, *with freedom.*

"But pure and holy, and as near to Thine own nature as aught can be to mortal eye, does this Thy Life flow forth as the bond which unites spirit with spirit, as the breath and atmosphere of a rational world, unimaginable and incomprehensible, and yet there, clearly visible to the spiritual eye. Borne onward in this stream of light, thought floats from soul to soul without pause or variation, and returns purer and brighter from each kindred mind. Through this mysterious union does each individual perceive, understand, and love himself only in another; each soul unfolds itself only through its fellows, and there are no longer individual men, but only one humanity; no individual thought or love or hate, but only thought, love and hate, in and through the other. Through this wondrous influence the affinity of spirits in the invisible world permeates even their physical nature;—manifests itself in two sexes, which, even if that spiritual bond could be torn asunder, would, simply as creatures of nature, be compelled to love each other;—flows forth in the tenderness of parents and children, brothers and sisters, as if the souls were of one blood like the bodies, and their minds were branches and blossoms of the same stem;—and from those embraces, in narrower or wider circles, the whole sentiment world. Even at the root of their hate, there lies a secret thirst after love; and no enmity springs up but from friendship denied.

"Through that which to others seems a mere dead mass, my eye beholds this eternal life and movement in every vein of sensible and spiritual Nature, and sees this life rising in ever-increasing growth, and ever purifying itself to a more spiritual expression. The universe is to me no longer what it was before—the ever-recurring circle, the eternally repeated play, the monster swallowing itself up only to bring itself forth again;—it has become transfigured before me, and now bears the one stamp of spiritual life—a constant progress toward higher perfection in a line that runs out into the Infinite.

"The sun rises and sets, the stars sink and reappear, the spheres hold their circle dance;—but they never return again as they disappeared, and even in the bright fountain of life itself there is life and progress. Every hour which they lead on, every morning and every evening, sinks with new increase upon the world; new life and new love descends from the spheres like dew-drops from the clouds, and encircle nature as the cool night the earth.

"All Death in Nature is Birth, and in Death itself appears visibly the exaltation of Life. There is no destructive principle in Nature, for Nature throughout is pure, unclouded Life; it is not Death that kills, but the more living Life which, concealed behind the former, bursts forth into new development. Death and Birth are but the struggle of Life with itself to assume a more glorious and congenial form. And *my* death,—how can it be aught else, since I am not a mere show, and semblance of life, but bear within me the original, true and essential Life? It is impossible to conceive that Nature should annihilate a life which does not proceed from her;—the Nature which exists for me and not I for her.

"Yet even my natural life, even this mere outward manifestation to mortal sight of the inward invisible Life, she cannot destroy without destroying herself;—she who only exists for me, and on account of me, and exists not if I am not. Even because she destroys me must she animate me anew; it is only my Higher Life, unfolding itself in her, before which my present life can disappear, and what mortals call Death is the visible appearance of this second Life. Did no reasonable being who had once beheld the light of this world die, there would be no ground to look with faith for a new heaven, and a new earth; the only possible purpose of Nature, to manifest and maintain Reason, would be fulfilled here below, and her circle would be completed. But the very fact by which she consigns a free and independent being to death, is her own solemn entrance, intelligible to all Reason, into a region beyond this act itself, and beyond the whole sphere of existence which is thereby closed. Death is the ladder by which my spiritual vision rises to a new Life and a new Nature.

"Every one of my fellow-creatures who leaves this earthly brotherhood and whom, because he is my brother, my spirit cannot regard as annihilated, draws my thoughts after him beyond the grave;—he is still, and to him there belongs a place. While we mourn for him here below,—as in the dim realms of unconsciousness there might be mourning when a man bursts from them into the light of this world's sun,—above there is rejoicing that a man is born into that world, as we citizens of the earth receive with joy those who are born unto us. When I shall one day follow, it will be but joy for me; sorrow shall remain in the sphere I shall have left.

"The world on which but now I gazed with wonder passes away from before me and is withdrawn from my sight. With all the fullness of life, order, and increase which I beheld in it, it is yet but the curtain by which a world infinitely more perfect is concealed from me, and the germ from which that other world shall develop itself. MY FAITH looks behind this veil, and cherishes and animates this germ.

It sees nothing definite, but it awaits more than it can conceive here below, more than it will ever be able to conceive in all time.

"Thus do I live, thus am I, and thus am I unchangeable, firm and completed for all Eternity;—for this is no existence assumed from without,—it is my own true, essential Life and Being."

JOHANN GOTTLIEB FICHTE.

www.ingramcontent.com/pod-product-compliance
Lightning Source LLC
Chambersburg PA
CBHW022135160426
43197CB00009B/1294